𝕳istory of 𝔅oston 𝔖eries — 𝔑umber 𝔗hirteen   ISSN 0305-2079

D1808954

BOSTON
POLITICS AND THE SEA
1652 - 1674

by

A. A. GARNER

Published for the History of Boston Project

RICHARD KAY PUBLICATIONS

80 Sleaford Road, Boston, Lincolnshire PE21 8EU

1975

History of Boston Series

This series is designed to consist of individual papers and material relevant to the history of the town of Boston in the county of Lincolnshire in England. These papers – which may be short and published several to a booklet or long enough to justify booklets to themselves – will range widely over many aspects of the life of the town. Some indeed may deal mainly with people and events far removed from Boston, but only in so far as they have a relevance to the history of the town itself.

All the papers in this series will be contributed by individuals through the 'History of Boston Project', usually from the material that they will have accumulated towards the proposed eventual book *The History of Boston*. However, although all papers are the work of the individual authors, who retain full responsibility for their own contributions, every paper (other than reprints from the documents of history themselves) is submitted to a professional authority before acceptance. Whether or not the professional advice is accepted is the responsibility of the individual author but nothing will be published in this series which is thought to be historically inaccurate or in any other way unacceptable as a work of history.

© A. A. Garner 1975

ISBN 0 902662 63 5

ISSN 0305 — 2079

Consultant Emeritus in Local History to the History of Boston Project

Alan Rogers, M.A., Ph.D., F.R.Hist.S., F.S.A., Senior Lecturer in Medieval and Local History, Department of Adult Education, University of Nottingham. Editor of *Bulletin of Local History East Midlands Region*. Edited *The Making of Stamford* (1965); *Stability and Change: some aspects of N. and S. Rauceby in the Nineteenth Century* (1969). Author of *The Medieval Buildings of Stamford* (1970), *A History of Lincolnshire* (1970), *This Was Their World* (1972), and of several papers on aspects of Lincolnshire history. Chairman of the History of Lincolnshire Committee.

PREFACE

The contents of this booklet are presented as a complement to and continuation of my *Boston and the Great Civil War* 1642-1651 which appeared as volume VII of the History of Boston Series. It covers the time which saw the dismantling and close of that outstanding period of the town's history when it was famed as a centre of Puritanism, and also attempts to convey an impression of how it fared during the three great sea wars which England fought against the Dutch Republic.

In setting the stage I have devoted a chapter to sketching in briefly the main outlines of Boston's development and standing as a port after it became a borough and began to throw off the nostalgia of its medieval glory. This period both deserves and requires far greater research and study, but I hope that what little I have given will prove of some value to other investigators in this field.

As before, I must acknowledge my debt to Mr. R. E. Coley, Boston's last Town Clerk before that ancient office fell to local government reorganisation, and now its Chief Executive, for kindly allowing me access to the Corporation Archives. My thanks go to Miss B. E. Robinson, Borough Librarian before the recent changes, for her courtesy and assistance at all times, and also to the Rev. Mark Spurrell who read my original typescript and furnished much useful comment and criticism. In addition, Mr. John Creasey, Deputy Librarian of Dr. Williams's Library, London, Mr. Michael Tunnard, of Emsworth, Hants., and Mr. A. H. Holmes of Boston, all supplied me with information for which I am duly grateful. Any opinions expressed herein, or errors, are of course my own, although I have done my best to eliminate the latter.

A. A. Garner.

Grimsby.
1974.

The Author

From his researches into the involvement of Boston in the civil wars of the 17th century, which appeared as *Boston and the Great Civil War*, the seventh booklet in this series, Arthur Garner uncovered material which has led to this present volume. His researches into the Port Books, a source of information which seems largely to have been ignored heretofore, gives a valuable insight into the fortunes of the Port of Boston at this time.

Although still living in Grimsby the vicissitudes of local government re-organization have removed him from the county of Lincolnshire to that of South Humberside. His interest in Boston's History however remains unchanged and further researches are already being made into the lives and families of a number of well known Bostonians of the past. It is hoped that in due course this also will appear in the Series.

Acknowledgement

We are most grateful to Rev. J. M. Spurrell, M.A., for reading the original draft of this booklet and for his helpful advice thereon.

We are glad to acknowledge the help of the Hydrographic Dept. of the Ministry of Defence for *Fig.* 1, which is reproduced with the sanction of the controller of H.M.S.O. and of the Hydrographer of the Navy; National Portrait Gallery, London, for *Fig.* 2; The author for his drawings reproduced as *Figs.* 3, 4, and 8; and the Public Record Office for *Figs.* 7, (SP 45/11) and 9, (SP 29/314)

CONTENTS

ILLUSTRATIONS

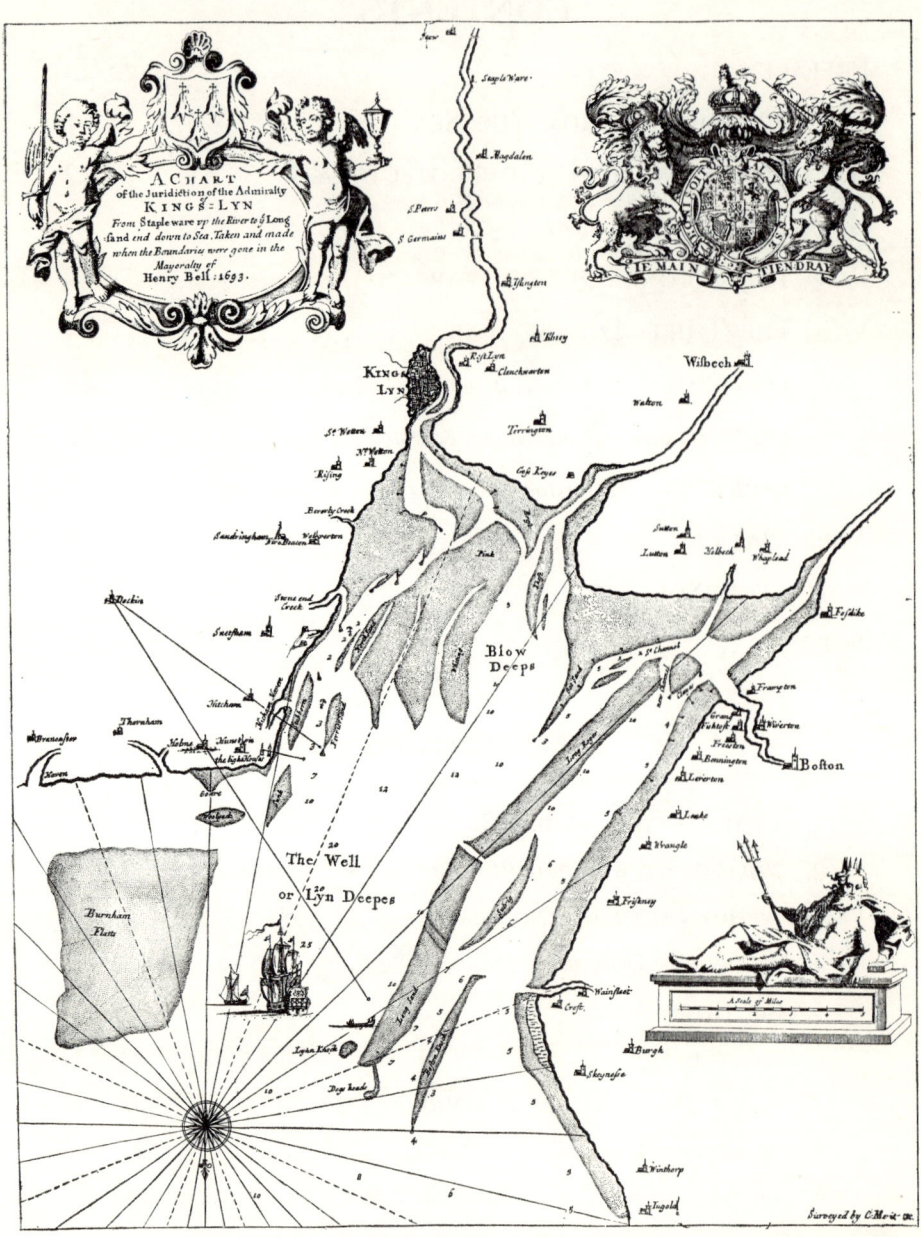

Fig. 1.

I. A PROSPECT FROM THE SEA

To appreciate Boston's standing as a town and port at the third quarter of the seventeenth century it is necessary to take a look at its earlier history, particularly that of the hundred years immediately preceding that period.

During the Middle Ages, Boston was a cosmopolitan trading centre whose wealth rivalled that of London. Wool export was the main pillar of its prosperity, and right on its doorstep in Lincolnshire and the fenlands around the Wash it had one of the richest producing areas of this commodity. During the reign of Edward I it was said that the wool of England amounted almost to the value of half of the whole land, and a third of the total exported at this time can be traced as going out through Boston.

Eventually however this lucrative trade declined and the port's golden era came to an end. By around the year 1541 when John Leland visited Boston its affluence was just a memory. He noted that the tide in the Haven ran 'sometymes as swifte as it were an arrow', but the Steelyard was deserted, and of the Hanseatic merchants who had once conducted thriving businesses there the only ones remaining were turning to dust in their tombs in the nearby Greyfriars.[1]

Leland had journeyed through an England wracked by Henry VIII's dissolution of the monasteries, and it was out of this great social upheaval that the Borough of Boston was born when in 1545 Henry sold to its community a parcel of confiscated townland and property, throwing in with the deal a charter of incorporation.

Scarce was the Corporation upon its feet however than it suffered a setback from the new boy-King, Edward VI, who under the Chantries Act sequestered from it 'diverse landes and tenements of a great yerely value' upon pretence that they had been 'concealed and wrongefullye deteyned' from the late King. This was in 1547. The loss was made good, but only after a lapse of seven years, when Philip and Mary made a

---

Fig. 1. (opposite) Chart of the Wash, published in 1693 and the earliest extant to show this section of the coast in detail. Drawn by Alderman Richard Bell of King's Lynn and based on a survey made by Christopher Merit, or Merret, M.D. and Surveyor of Boston. According to the latter (*Philosophical Transactions of the Royal Society*, vol. XIX, 1696, p.352) it was designed for inclusion in Greenvile Collins's *Great Britain's Coasting Pilot* but it does not appear in any of the several editions of that work which appeared between 1693 and 1792. This copy is preserved as survey A31Qf in the archives of the Hydrographic Department of the Ministry of Defence. Reproduced with the sanction of the Controller, HM Stationary Office and of the Hydrographer of the Navy. [see also inside back cover for details of availability of large scale version.]

royal grant of the so-called Erection Lands in 1554. As late as 1592 the intervening loss of income was played upon by the Corporation in obtaining tax relief from Elizabeth I. Also argued at the same time was the decayed state of the port, an example of how for at least 80 years after its inception the Corporation was regularly to invoke Boston's medieval eminence as a yardstick when petitioning for a concession or fending off taxation.[2]

The Corporation was a closed shop and monopoly organisation. It consisted of a mayor, twelve aldermen, eighteen common councillors, and employed a Recorder and other officials. A new mayor was chosen yearly from among the aldermen. Any deficiency in their number was filled from the common council, which in turn was recruited from the freemen. Freemanship was attainable through apprenticeship to a freeman for seven years plus payment of a small admission fee, or by straight purchase for a sum that initially varied but was later stabilised at £5; a level that effectually closed that avenue to any but the well off. In the latter instance the goodwill of the Corporation was of course a prerequisite.

Except for the supplying of victuals and dealings during annual fair days the right to practice commerce in the borough was confined to the freemen. The port jurisdiction embraced the 'precincts of the Deeps of Boston, extending even to a place called Saltney Yates', probably Fosdyke Creek. Inside that limit no vessel, upon pain of forfeiture, could load or unload without licence from the Corporation, which also enjoyed many other rights and privileges. The openings for corruption and abuse in such a set-up were manifold, but it was to stand, basically unaltered, for three hundred years until remodelled by the Municipal Corporations Reform Act of 1835.[3]

In June 1571 a law came into effect[4] which restricted the export of grain, and this led to a new turning in Boston's port history when in November the Corporation reacted by deciding to apply for a special and profitable export licence to transport 6,000 quarters of grain, coupling with it a request for a Royal Loan of £1,000 to be repaid in six years.[5]

Nothing more is heard of the loan, but the Corporation, represented in London by Alderman Christopher Audley, continued to press for the licence, soliciting the aid of friends in the Privy Council. Its case appears to have been that the port was becoming derelict for want of finance, and that ships were avoiding it because of its hazardous unmarked approaches. The friends referred to were Sir William 'Mr. Secretary' Cecil, and Edward, Lord Clinton, both courtiers of Lincolnshire antecedents and with considerable influence. Cecil was in the lengthy process of erecting Burghley House, the magnificent dwelling near Stamford which now delights the visiting public at large. The Recordership of Boston, which he had held since May 1551,[6] was but a minor pendant to his chain of important offices and preferments. Clinton was Lord High Admiral of England and shortly to be first Earl of Lincoln. His son, Sir Henry Clinton of Tattershall, from whose estates the Corporation had already contracted for timber to repair its port facilities,[7] was Vice-Admiral of

2

Fig. 2. William Cecil, Lord Burghley. Recorder of Boston from 1551 to 1598. Painting attributed to Marcus Gheeraerts the Younger. National Portrait Gallery, London.

Lincolnshire and High Steward of Boston, a post which Lord Clinton had held earlier.

Nevertheless, Boston's suit was slow to prosper. It may be surmised that a prime difficulty was the aged William Paulet, Marquis of Winchester and Lord High Treasurer. He was not then on good terms with Cecil, and furthermore he would only have to refer to recent copies of Boston's Port Books, annually deposited with his department, to see that although the town was far from flourishing, the Corporation's lament that it was 'destitute of ships and trade of shipping' was an exaggeration.

Taking the two years of the negotiations, 1571-72, an examination of the books for Michaelmas 1570 to Michaelmas 1571 shows 72 inward and 35 outward loggings of coastal shipping. Just over half of the incoming were Newcastle colliers. In addition there are 38 entries relating to the arrival and departure of foreign or overseas traders. These include Scottish vessels. For Michaelmas 1571 to Michaelmas 1572 no coastal books survive, but the overseas trade was on a par with that of the previous year. Boston was importing French wine, general cargo from Germany (Hamburg), and salt, fish, and linen from ports on the Firth of Forth. Its exports were predominantly sheepskins, wool, hides, and leather.[8] The port owned seven active ships,[9] only two of which engaged in overseas trade.

Consequently, the Queen's Council appear to have used the licence as a bargaining counter, making its granting conditional upon the Corporation implementing a degree of developmental self-help by purchasing for £100 a Charter of Admiralty which would greatly increase its powers and advantages. There was however also some talk of the reversion of the stewardship of the town and the administration of its income, and the Corporation, not wanting interlopers, ordered Audley on 31 January 1572 to suspend proceedings until these aspects could be resolved to its full advantage.[10] Matters then hung fire for almost three months, and it is significant that in this time Paulet died and Cecil was created Baron Burghley and lined up for the vacant Treasurership. On April 18, Audley and three other aldermen were instructed by the Corporation to reapply for the grain licence and to 'opteyne and gett to the use of the said mayor and burgesses and to their successors the holl authoritie and Jurisdiccion of the Admyraltie within the said Borough and liberties of the same'.[11]

Both requests were duly filled, the Admiralty Charter bearing the date 10 February 1573. It greatly supplemented the powers contained in the Henrician charter, and among its several provisions the Corporation gained admiralty control of over thirty miles of coast with its creeks and inlets, from Wainfleet to the Norfolk border, and seawards over the whole north-western half of the Wash, in which it undertook to place seamarks for the guidance and safety of mariners. A specified scale of tolls was to be levied upon those who benefited by these. A weekly Admiralty Court to be presided over by a qualified person appointed by the Corporation ensured that it received its share of the profits arising out of shipwreck, salvage, and other marine law-suits arising within its area. The Corpora-

4

tion also had full rights to so-called royal fishes; 'Sturgeons, Whales, Porpoises, Dolphins, Riggs and Grampusses and all other fishes having in them any great fatness and thickness'. The Crown reserved the right to infringe the Charter in time of war.[12]

Three days after the Charter grant, the Queen issued a licence for forty families of Dutch fishermen to settle in the borough, apparently to stimulate the growth of a fishing industry there. The idea does not appear to have taken root, for a publication of 1614 makes particular remark of the dearth of fishing in Boston.[13]

The grain licence originally applied for was issued on 18 February 1573 and allowed the export of 20,000 quarters of grain within the counties of Lincoln and Norfolk over a period of five years at a preferentially reduced duty payable of 8d. per quarter. The Corporation used it with an enthusiasm that had by May created a local shortage and price inflation; a situation that obliged Burghley to forward a letter of reprimand.[14] To the end of his life however this great Elizabethan statesman was to display a paternal interest in the borough. In 1576 he was instrumental in getting some of its inhabitants admitted to London's exclusive Company of Merchant Adventurers, and in 1580 the Mayor and Burgesses found that their 'singular good lord' smiled upon a request for renewal of the grain licence, necessary for the repair, yet again, of their 'decayed wharves and staythes'.[15] Lest it be thought however that all was now continuing sweetness and light in the port's administration, in 1593 he was called upon to arbitrate over a petition from Boston's Customs Officers against the Corporation, which they claimed was overriding their authority for making seizures of contraband, and damaging trade by maltreating and forcing out alien merchants. Also the Vice-Admiral of the county and his deputies were doing more or less as they liked in the port. The Corporation responded that the customers were young, inexperienced, and guilty of slander. It agreed about the Vice-Admiral, lugubriously pointing out that this was a sample of how it was put upon by high and low alike![16]

The Corporation had often to assert its Charter rights, as in 1605 when it doggedly pursued an expensive litigation over custody of a stranded whale. Burghley being then deceased, it had to apply to his two sons in order to obtain satisfaction.[17] Thomas, Earl of Exeter, the eldest of these, had taken up the patent for Recordership of the borough at his father's death.[18]

The charter obligation to place navigation aids in the Boston Deeps was farmed out by the Corporation in May 1574 for a span of 21 years to its negotiator, Christopher Audley. He received £20 for launching expenses, was to pay an annual fee of 2s. to the Corporation, and stood bound to it in the sum of £100 to perfect a system of 'bekons, boyes and cannes'. In return he was entitled to the tolls accruing; a small return in his case, for he died in the following year.[19] That the undertaking was eventually realised is evidenced by an entry in the Corporation Minutes for 1580 which gives a detailed account of a survey of the seamarks.[20]

Boston's sister port, King's Lynn, received an Admiralty Charter from James I in 1604. Similar in content to that of Boston, it encompassed the remaining sea area and coastline of the Wash not ceded to Boston's authority.[21] In 1663, in order to prevent shipwrecks, 183 of the inhabitants of both ports, being shipowners, masters, and others, petitioned the King for permission to erect lights on Hunstanton Cliff. This was granted in 1665, and soon after, two lighthouses, estimated to have cost £210, were constructed. Thus it can be seen that the period outlined above was one which witnessed the introduction of a serious and steadily improving provision for the order and safety of Wash traffic, a process in which Boston played a leading part. Nevertheless, it seems that there may have been instances of neglectful backsliding along the way, as in 1660 we find 18 of Boston's mariners petitioning the Corporation 'in regard of want of boyes laid in convenient places'.[22]

Some impression of Boston's trade standing, in relation to other English ports towards the beginning of the seventeenth century, can be gained from a document preserved among the Cecil MSS.[23] It lists eighteen ports (excluding London) and the total customs duty derived from each for the year 1595. Boston stands fourteenth with a return of £111.12s.6½d. directly after King's Lynn, showing £282.19s.0½d. Of seven east coast ports given, Boston is lowest, with Sandwich (£3,125 18s.2½d.) and Hull (£2,130.17s.8½d.) the highest. The four ports lower than Boston in the full list are all on the west coast. However, another source which strikes the average customs return from several ports over the next five years, Michaelmas 1596 to Michaelmas 1601, shows that while Hull and Lynn maintained about the same level of return during this time, that of Boston underwent a rise to £1,684.9s.3d.[24]

Whatever the cause of this, it appears to have vanished as abruptly as it came. A computation of the duties recorded in the overseas trade Port Books of Boston which survive for the period Michaelmas 1601 – Christmas 1640, recently published under the editorship of Dr. R. W. K. Hinton, indicates that between 1601-2 and 1613 they ranged from £62.9s.4d. in 1601-2 to a peak of £149.19s.3d. in 1610. For 1615 and 1617 the average was £277, while 1618 yielded £140.7s.10½d. The years 1630-40 were boom years in terms of trade carried in English and particularly Boston-owned shipping in which 1633 topped £260 and in 1639 reached £403.8s.3½d.[25] During this time the Corporation, predictably, brought its 'decayed port' routine into play when confronted with Charles I's demand for Ship Money.[26]

For the Civil War and Interregnum no detailed port trade information for Boston is available. What is forthcoming of its involvement in the strife has already been given,[27] and this is sufficient to show that as a port it had a significant role. Unfortunately its Port Books, from 1640 to 1660, a source of great potential value, were either lapsed or have disappeared. From a list of customs revenue under the Commonwealth, expressed in round figures, it appears that in 1649-50 Boston returned £400.[28] Regarding the Corporation's internal finances, i.e. rents from property and

6

market stalls, Fair profits, and Mart proceeds, G. M. Hipkin has demonstrated that they suffered little if any dislocation; an exception being the Mart return for 1642-3 when the war came closest to Boston.[29]

For the period 1660-74, overseas trade port books for Boston exist for the latter half of 1660 and for the whole of 1661, 1667, 1668, 1670, and 1673.[30] Out of a possible eighteen books for these years (one each annually for three customs officers)[31] ten survive. Subject to the deterioration and damage that three centuries have visited upon them they divulge enough information to suggest that the shipping boom of the 1630's was either maintained or recovered. Out of a total of 45 inward and outward loggings of shipping in the six months of 1660, 25 apply to English ships, 17 of them Boston owned. It is emphasised that these figures relate to the employment of ships, not their number. For the whole of 1661 the total is 78; 50 being English, 36 Boston owned. In 1668 and 1670 the figures are 52:43:34 and 66:50:39 respectively. During 1667 and 1673 the port appears to have suffered a recession, no doubt due to the sea wars against the Dutch. In a total of 26 entries recoverable from a port book of the former year, only 7 concern English ships, and all these belonged to Boston. In 1673 the total is 27 against 5 English, 3 being of Boston. Even so, the custom obtained in this year is reckonable as £5,155.14s.8¾d., being levied under the heads of coinage duty, additional duty, subsidy, and impost.[32] The sum clearly shows the considerable increase in this form of taxation that had taken place since the outbreak of the Civil War.[33]

The names of at least 26 Boston ships are traceable as operating during 1660-73[34] and various references in the State Papers make it possible to identify the port's merchantmen of the seventeenth century as being of the types known as pinks, ketches, hoys*, and doggers.[35] Taken from the port books, 1601-73, they appear to have ranged in burthen from 8 to a maximum of 120 tons. From the same source it may be mentioned in passing that the vessel of biggest burthen recorded to have docked in the Haven during this period was in 1601, the *Royal Merchant* of London at 200 tons, in from the Italian port of Leghorn.[36]

Apart from coast-wise traffic, Boston's ships traded with Norway and along the continental littoral between points as widespread as the Gulf of Danzig in the east to (in one instance, the *Unicorn* in 1613) Lisbon in the west. By far the commonest ports regularly visited were Rotterdam and Amsterdam. A sampling of ten voyages there from Boston and back again, carried out during 1639-40 by three ships, the *Post*, *Content*, and *Fortune*, shows an average round trip time of 52 days. 'Turnaround' in Boston averaged 37 days. The *Unicorn* referred to above was logged out to Lisbon, a distance of some 1300 nautical miles on September 15, and in again from Bordeaux on December 6, an absence of 81 days.[37]

The exports carried in Boston's ships reflected the economy of its surrounding district. The oil-bearing seeds of rape, cole, and hemp, all

---

* See *Fig*. 3. p.8, Also *Fig*. 4. p.13, and *Fig*. 8. p.33.

fen-grown plants, some already processed into oil-cakes, figure largely. Ladings of butter, hides, horsehair, and glue lend weight to the hint given by William Camden in 1586 that the local inhabitants made a good living out of grazing, and the claim of the pamphleteer 'Anti-Projector' in 1606 that the fens bred 'infinite numbers of serviceable horses, mares and colts'.[38] Lead, much exported after 1660, doubtless came from the mines of the Derbyshire High Peak.

Fig. 3.

- *Hoy* -

Imports were timber from Scandinavia, of which a considerable quantity was brought in in 1661 and 1670,[39] while from the Low Countries a multiplicity of general cargo included such goods as steel, iron, paper, whale-oil, earthenware, copper and brass vessels, flax, glass, rice, and starch. From Bordeaux came wines and brandy and their associated items, prunes, currants, and vinegar. Perry, a beverage obtained from pears, also appears after 1660. Rosin, another import from Bordeaux, probably came from the great forests of the Landes, south of the Gironde, where the trees are still tapped for this product.

Concerning the origin and mode of ownership of Boston's ships, some light is thrown by entries in the Controller's port book for 1661. In February the *John and Thomas*, burthen 30 tons, was registered as belonging to the port, having been purchased in Rotterdam. The customs office valued it at £80. It was owned jointly by its master, Edward Mallery, and merchants John Atkin, Samuel Browne, and Thomas Truse. In July the *John and Elizabeth*, 30 tons, was booked as bought in Rotterdam from Adrean Soulderwagen. James Sneath, master and co-owner with John Atkin and Samuel Beetson, merchants, confirmed on oath to the customers that it cost £100.[40]

8

A study of the merchants' names in the overseas trade port books 1660-73 reveals the same picture as that to which attention has been drawn elsewhere[41] in regard to the books for 1601-40; namely that the Corporation was heavily represented. The ship-masters on the other hand, notwithstanding their importance to the town's well-being, seem to have been content to remain an aloof fraternity. In the whole period under review only two, Samuel Burdis, master of the *Elizabeth* in 1660-68, and William Otter, master of the *John* in 1660-62, are readily discernible as having entered local politics. The former was a common councillor and the latter an alderman, both in 1662.[42]

While acquisition from outside sources would doubtless account for the origin of the majority of Boston's ships, the question of whether any were built in Boston naturally follows. Dr. Hinton considers the matter without reaching any firm conclusion,[43] but, although the port would certainly be no Clydeside, there is in fact some evidence to indicate that before about 1646 ships were built there. It comes in a letter written in 1666 by Daniel Rhodes, who was Mayor in that year and ordered by the Navy Commissioners to impress shipwrights for work in the royal dockyards. He replied that no ship had been built in Boston for the previous twenty years and that there was only one artisan among the inhabitants and he had not exercised his trade for ten years. Boatwrights were available, but Rhodes judged them 'altogether unfit for works upon the King's ships'[44]

The various craft industries ancillary to ships and the sea would undoubtedly be well represented in Boston. There is proof that one, rope-making, certainly was. On a spring day in St. James's Park in 1672 Sir Anthony Irby, Boston's M.P., button-holed the navy's surveyor-general, Mr. Samuel Pepys, and told him of a neighbour of his in Boston who would undertake to make up very good cordage of Riga hemp.[45] This was probably a certain James Clarke, who first appears in 1651 as factor for shipping supplies from Boston to Cromwell's army in Scotland. During 1653-55 he filled naval contracts from both Boston and King's Lynn for converting native and foreign hemp into cordage, and also in this period he reported to the Navy Commissioners on having sent carpenters out from Boston to the woods to fell and shape timber into masts, sixty of which he had purchased, each of 24 inches in diameter.[46]

Pepys had earlier, in 1663, investigated the price and quality of Lincolnshire hemp through one of his agents, who reported on having taken samples at Boston where there was 'a good quantity grown'. According to a writer of 1652 the best hemp in England was grown in the Holland division of the county.[47] Boston's Corporation Minutes make reference in 1611 to provisions for marketing it in the town.[48] The great acreage of it grown in the fens eventually decreased, and it finally disappeared in the early nineteenth century.

TABLE BASED ON BOSTON'S SURVIVING OVERSEAS TRADE PORT BOOKS FOR THE PERIOD 1601 - 1674 [OPPOSITE]

A dash indicates that the relevant information is not recorded in the source. Figures asterisked are qualified by remarks given in the appended explanatory note below.

EXPLANATORY NOTE

In the first column the abbreviation Mch. indicates that the year runs from Michaelmas to Michaelmas. Chr. denotes Christmas to Christmas. Mds:Chr. is a half year, Midsummer to Christmas.

The total of customs duty returned for the year, given in column two, is expressed to the nearest £. It will be noticed that for five of the years listed no figure is given. With the exception of 1660-61 the reason for this is the fact that the only surviving port book for the year is that of the Searcher; entries of duty paid being confined to the books kept by the other two officers, the Controller and the Customer. The year 1660-61 marks a departure from usual practice. Here the only book extant is that of the Controller, but nevertheless it contains no record of duty. Totals asterisked are the best obtainable in view of the damage sustained by the books from which they derive; particularly bad in the case of 1667-68. The sum of £1427 given for 1669-70 is for six months only. For this year the books of the Searcher and Controller are available but the latter's entries terminate in June 1670.

Column three gives the total of inward and outward loggings of vessels using the port during the year. We are therefore here concerned with the employment of ships and not their actual number. Totals asterisked are complete as far as damage to the port books will allow. The ensuing columns grouped under 'Ship Nationality' and 'Countries of trading' are based on a breakdown of this initial figure.

The column 'Greatest tons burthen' gives the maximum recorded tonnage of any ship appearing in the port during the year.

In the four columns grouped under 'Boston ships' we are dealing with the actual number of Boston owned ships evident in the port books for each year. The asterisked figures 60 and 40 in 1610-11 and 1615-16 respectively are not the average tonnage as stated at the head of the column, but the burthen of the third Boston ship. Eight Boston ships are traceable in the half year of 1660 but the tonnages of only three are recorded. These are the three asterisked figures which follow.

10

YEAR	Total Customs Duty (£)	Total ship loggings incoming & outgoing	Ship Nationality			Countries of trading						Greatest tons burthen	Boston Ships			
			Foreign (inc. Scotland)	English (inc. Boston owned)	Boston owned	Scotland	Low Countries	Norway	France	Others	Record illegible		Number	Maximum tons burthen	Minimum tons burthen	Average tons burthen
Mch. 1601-02	62	32	24	8	4	18	7	2	1	4	0	200	2	40	30	—
Mch. 1602-03	121	42	34	8	6	31	5	2	3	0	1	100	4	40	10	29
Mch. 1604-05	105	36	24	12	6	16	7	5	4	4	0	70	4	37	16	29
Chr. 1609-10	150	26	15	11	5	-	-	-	-	-	-	-	5	-	-	-
Chr. 1610-11	106	48	36	12	7	13	18	10	5	2	0	70	3	70	24	60*
Chr. 1611-12	102	38	20	18	8	11	12	4	5	6	0	80	4	70	6	46
Chr. 1612-13	92	40	33	7	3	19	8	6	4	3	0	70	1	70	-	-
Chr. 1614-15	221	69	58	11	6	19	31	8	6	2	3	100	2	50	30	-
Chr. 1615-16	-	82	74	8	6	16	55	4	3	2	2	80	3	50	32	40*
Chr. 1616-17	233	57	50	7	3	14	33	4	5	0	1	100	1	50	-	-
Chr. 1617-18	140	36	28	8	6	11	16	4	2	1	2	80	5	50	20	33
Chr. 1627-28	-	21	4	17	17	0	18	3	0	0	0	160	6	60	26	43
Chr. 1629-30	242	18	9	9	8	1	6	9	1	0	1	120	5	120	26	69
Chr. 1632-33	260	42	9	33	28	3	18	10	7	4	0	140	9	120	20	54
Chr. 1633-34	236*	51	16	35	22	1	20	15	7	8	0	120	9	90	16	46
Chr. 1638-39	403*	58	19	39	32	2	32	14	7	3	0	100	10	50	8	27
Chr. 1639-40	-	59	21	38	30	0	32	16	5	5	1	100	11	90	12	37
Mds:Chr. 1660	-	45	20	25	17	5	12	13	2	2	11	60	8	30*	20*	20*
Chr. 1660-61	-	78	28	50	36	4	25	35	10	0	4	70	8	36	20	28
Chr. 1666-67	745*	26*	19	7	7	1	10	4	2	1	8	-	6	-	-	-
Chr. 1667-68	1770*	52*	9	43	34	0	26	13	10	1	2	-	12	-	-	-
Chr. 1669-70	1427*	66	16	50	39	2	25	27	8	1	3	-	11	-	-	-
Chr. 1672-73	5156	27	22	5	3	0	6	14	7	0	0	-	3	-	-	-

II. COMMONWEALTH & PROTECTORATE

At the beginning of 1652 Boston's Civil War garrison, after a life of some nine years, had just been disbanded.[49] Charles II, pursued out of the country after his defeat in battle at Worcester on 3 September 1651 was residing in exile on the continent, and England was entering its fourth year as a Commonwealth ruled by a Council of State and the Rump of the Long Parliament.

The English Republic, though destined to be short-lived, was a lusty creation whose aggressive foreign policy was to result in war, first with Holland and then with Spain. The war with the Dutch was the first of three which England was to undertake against that formidable sea-going nation. The second and third took place after the Restoration and their effects upon Boston will be dealt with in chapters IV and V. Maritime and commercial jealousy was the spur to all of them. The Dutch had built up a monopoly of the world's carrying trade which England was determined to break while also forcing its rival to salute the flag in the Narrow Seas in perpetual acknowledgment of England's naval supremacy.

The fuse was lit in October 1651 with the passing of the Navigation Act which forbade the import of any goods into England except in English ships or in ships of the producing country. War exploded into being in May 1652 and the form it took set the pattern for the wars which came later; namely that while the opposing navies pounded each other in set battles in the Channel and North Sea, the English coast, particularly the eastern seaboard, became the happy hunting ground of privateers and pirates.

For Boston and other maritime communities this meant years of depression, trouble, and anxiety. Raiding was well under way months before the formal opening of hostilities, as shown by a letter of 15 December 1651 from the Council of State to the Navy Commissioners which states that Boston and Lynn were suffering heavily from piracy, and therefore the Council had contracted through James Clarke for the hire of a 'nimble vessel' for protection purposes. It was the *Concord* of Yarmouth, of 100 tons and 40 men. Captain Edward Mould, 'a man well experienced on that coast' was to command her.[50] He was a Boston shipmaster whose name appears often in the Port Books for 1628-40.

The rapid falling off of Boston's commerce is attested by an entry in the Corporation Minutes, dated 2 November 1652, which abates Mary Bonner, widow, of payment of £12.10s., her rental of the farm of the port tolls, because of the 'present great decay of the shipping and trade of this Borough occasioned by the great warres now at sea between the English and the Dutch'.[51]

12

Matters were worsened by the pressing of able seamen into the Navy. Henry Rosse of the *Trial* of Boston was one of several shipmasters who complained to the authorities on this score. Deprived of all his crew he was left stranded at Gravesend with goods worth £10,000 for Boston's Fair.[52]

The protection afforded by the *Concord* was supplemented by that of a navy frigate, the *Briar*. The services of the latter were withdrawn early in 1653 but soon restored following an outcry from Boston and Lynn.[53] It was a ship that one Boston man later had cause to remember with regret. He was Thomas Ridley, master of the Boston dogger *Providence*. On the night of 13 March 1654, on charter to London merchants with a cargo of rapeseed and lead, he was in convoy from Hull to St. Valery in France when he was run down and sunk by the *Briar*. The total value of the loss was £700, of which his share was £300. Pleading the ruination of himself and his family he claimed compensation, and after some deliberation a naval court absolved him of blame in the accident and awarded him the grant of a prize vessel to the value of £150. Out of this he eventually obtained a cheaper vessel, the *Ellen*, together with a number of ships' guns to make up the difference.[54]

Fig. 4.

- *Dogger* -

On 23 April 1654 a Boston ship was reported as taken off the Yorkshire coast[55] although the war was by then over, ended by treaty almost three weeks earlier. The Dutch fleet had been brilliantly led by Van Tromp, one of the greatest admirals of the age, but it had nevertheless been battered into submission by that of England under the direction of an even greater naval genius, Robert Blake. Flushed with victory and imbued with a resurgence of the Elizabethan tradition, the Protectoral government then turned its sea power against Catholic Spain, menacing it in the Mediterranean and striking at its plate fleets and colonies in the Caribbean.

This change of front simply took the east coast ports out of the frying pan and into the fire, for the attentions of Dutch privateers gave place to those of Flemish and Biscayan corsairs operating from the fortresses of Dunkirk and Ostend in the Spanish Netherlands. Counter measures involved the seaward blockade of these strong-holds and later their siege on land by allied Anglo-French forces. Convoying was continued, and the State Papers contain references to Boston shipping movements under this protection. Cargoes of naval victuals and ammunition are mentioned.[56]

Despite all, the privateers could not be suppressed completely. Like their predecessors the Dutch had done, and would do again, they exploited to the full an advantage which was pointed out by the Mayor of King's Lynn, writing to a member of the Privy Council in January 1657. In reporting the capture of a Boston hoy he emphasized that the enemy were peace-time traders to the area and therefore had an intimate knowledge of the coast.[57]

Prisoners taken by both sides were repatriated by exchange. In April 1657 the Mayor of York received a letter from Joseph, Jeremy, and Thomas Waller, Thomas Moore, and William Pinchbeck, captives in Ostend. They were all Boston men, the crew of one of the port's colliers, by whose seizure they had sustained a loss of £1,000. They asked that some of the enemy held in York Castle be offered in exchange.[58]

In another Ostend letter, a month later, Thomas Ball, master of a Boston hoy, solicited the aid of a London merchant to obtain the names of two prisoners, 'married men if possible to enlist the aid of their wives', for like exchange. He also needed the name of a boy for Jonathan Bonde, his apprentice. Ball cautioned his correspondent that the prisoners should not be cleared until he was released. 'If you write to Boston remember me home' he concluded wistfully. It seems that the hopes of these men may have been frustrated. Two years later nine shipmasters, some of Boston, reminded the Admiralty Commissioners that they were still prisoners and begged for consideration.[59]

We turn now to the borough's internal affairs. Boston had been staunchly Roundhead during the Civil War, and after the execution of Charles I in 1649, an event which alienated many powerful moderate supporters from the Parliament's side, the town had maintained its anti-Royalist stance.[60] At the beginning of February 1653, pursuant to orders received, its charters were forwarded to London for examination so that their validity under the Commonwealth could be confirmed.[61] It was purely a formality for a study of the Corporation Minutes over the whole of the Interregnum period reveals no change in the Corporation's composition, its administrative machinery, nor business proceedings. With its liberties unimpaired it was content to support or acquiesce (and indeed it is difficult to see how it could have done any other) in the various efforts made up to 1660 to establish the government of England on a permanent non-monarchical basis.

14

In religion too the indications are that the town retained its renowned puritanism, something that would naturally commend it to the regime. In 1654 it supplied six commissioners for the county implementation of the resoundingly titled Ordinance for Ejecting Scandalous, Ignorant and Insufficient Ministers and Schoolmasters,[62] a measure aimed at suppressing Episcopal minded clergy and others whose preachings were considered subversive or distasteful by the government.

When in 1656 the founder of Quakerism, George Fox, made a proselytising visit, Boston took him in its stride. His doctrine with its anarchistic overtones was singled out for general condemnation even in an age that had digested many bizarre religious sects, and the appearance of its followers in a town was frequently the signal for mischief from the hooligan element and persecution from the authorities. With an entourage he had just come from Crowland where he had been roughly handled by the vicar and his clerk. Fox records that at Boston, apart from a 'raving man', soon quieted, in the yard of the inn where he stayed, there was no trouble. Most of the principal inhabitants came to hear him speak and 'ye people seemed to bee much satisfyed . . . & some was convinct there alsoe'.[63] Two years later when one of his disciples, John Whitehead, put in an appearance, the town was in a less accommodating mood, for Whitehead wound up in its jail.[64]

Boston's outlook was again manifest when a religious row broke out in the summer of 1658. It was provoked by Hugh Wyndham, a circuit judge then sitting at Lincoln Assizes. A number of clergymen were arraigned before him after he had ruled that it was lawful for parishioners to refuse tithes to a minister who would not baptise the children of, or administer the Sacrament to, any who would not pin their faith to their sleeve. He was also said to have declared that in this respect these ministers 'dealt worse with the people than the Popish priests, who would allow to all'. It was the chronically festering Royalist-Parliamentarian religious ulcer flaring up again, Such views, however tolerant and civilised, were anathema to the puritan precept of 'separating the precious from the vile' and an indignant county petition was promptly fired off to the Lord Protector, pleading that Wyndham be discredited. The signatures of John Tooley, Boston's current mayor, and five of its leading citizens headed the list of 38 subscribed names. Wyndham was put out of his office, but he regained it after the Restoration and was later knighted.[65]

Constant as Boston's religious bias may have been, there were probably many of its inhabitants during these troubled years who were unhappy with the political impasse into which the nation had fallen. Those avowedly or secretly Royalist, together with Parliamentarian moderates, would have watched the sad train or events that had produced a military dictatorship with the country divided into regions administered by Major-Generals, and yearned longingly for a return to the basic constitutional stability of the pre-war years. There might well also have been others, Republicans or Levellers from the left wing of the puritan movement, who disliked the regime because they saw it as an obstacle to the setting up of a more democratic social order.

Numbered among Boston's dissidents we could expect to find members of the Thorold family. They were among the very few in the community who had taken up arms for the King and had been subsequently penalised for it. Sir Anthony Irby, a leading resident, was undoubtedly discontented. As M.P. for the borough since 1628 he had sided with the Parliament until his seclusion from the House by the Army at Pride's Purge in 1648. A Puritan of the Presbyterian variety he was no enemy to the institution of monarchy, having sought only to curb its excesses. We also hear, in 1655, of words spoken against the Protector by Joseph Whiting, of Boston, being referred to Edward Whalley, Lincolnshire's Major-General, although on examination Whalley reported no case to answer. Whiting was Corporation tenant of the land occupied by and adjoining the still extant Hussey Tower. He came from a prestigious local family of wool-dealers, and his father and grand-father had between them held the mayoralty of the borough on six occasions. His uncle, Samuel Whiting, was a puritan cleric who in 1636 had followed John Cotton to America. [66]

Between 1650 and 1660 there were four major national designs, all abortive, engineered by the Royalists and their allies to reseat Charles II upon his throne, and in each Boston had a place; an indication of its considered military value and/or hinting at the expectation that help would be forthcoming from within once the die was cast. The town's part in the first two, in 1650 and 1651, has already been covered; [67] the third came to a head in 1655 and the government had known of its maturing and the threat to Boston long before that. Accordingly, in June 1654, companies from the foot regiment of Major-General John Lambert were stationed in the town. [68] We can be sure that this unit was carefully chosen, for Lambert was a strong and trusted protagonist of Cromwell, and the Lord Protector knew that at Belleau, 25 miles north of Boston, there dwelt in retirement a remarkable individual who was probably the most able and resourceful politician in England; a man who had stood in the Commons and cried shame on him, when, supported by Lambert and his soldiers he had forcibly disbanded the Rump Parliament in April 1653.

This was Sir Henry Vane, late M.P. for Hull. He had purchased the manor of Belleau in 1651 out of the sequestered estate of the Royalist Earl of Lindsey, [69] and the measure of his political standing can be assessed from his having been said to be, during the Civil War, 'within the House what Cromwell was without'. A Puritan of note (he had been Governor of Massachusetts at the age of 22 and a close companion of John Cotton) his views on religion were highly complex and expressed in such laby-rinthine terms as to be almost incomprehensible even to his learned contemporaries. This caused the satirist Thomas Flatman to dub him 'Knight of the Mysterious Allegories', and his style may still be appreciated in surviving documents which include four letters written to his friend Richard Cust, son of Samuel Cust of Boston. [70] Despite its obscurity his peculiar theology appealed to many, among them being Lambert's wife, Frances, who became one of his followers. [71] She may have lived for some

16

Fig. 5.   Sir Henry Vane (from *Life and Death of Sir Henry Vane* by George Sikes, 1662.)

time either at Belleau or Boston, as in May 1654 the Mayor's Accounts record 16s. 8d. expended on making her a gift.[72]

Politically, Vane was a Republican and had strong Lincolnshire ties binding him into the great cousinage of its Parliamentarian families. His wife, Frances Wray, was niece to Sir Anthony Irby's first wife, and this in turn related him to the powerful Ayscough clan and many others.[73] Being aware of this, and Vane's consummate skill in reconciling factions to attain his ends, Cromwell must have pondered uneasily upon what trouble might be brewed for him in this corner of England.

Lincolnshire offices held by Vane included those of J.P., militia commissioner, and Vice-Admiral of the county; the latter not surprisingly

17

since he was of vast experience in naval administration, having been eminently concerned with it since 1639. Boston's Corporation probably had its port interest well in mind when we find it, between 1652 and 1657, frequently plying him with presents of fish, wine, and sugar. He is said to have stood for a county seat in the first Protectorate Parliament of 1654 and a list of the period gives him as for Grimsby, but the member there was William Wray and there is no note of a poll in its archives. In 1656 he was rumoured to have tried for a seat at Boston, though by that time Cromwell had judged it prudent to have him temporarily locked away on the Isle of Wight. At the Restoration Vane was a marked man. He was not a regicide but was arraigned for high treason and in court defended his past conduct with such disturbing and fearless eloquence that the King was moved to suggest that he was 'too dangerous to let live if we can honestly put him out of the way'. Sir Henry's head duly fell on Tower Hill on 14 June 1662.[74]

In common with all boroughs except London, Boston sent no member to the 'Barebones' Parliament or 'Assembly of the Saints' of 1653, but one of the five persons nominated to represent Lincolnshire was Richard Cust. A tract which was circulated classifies him as politically of the 'Advanced' Party as opposed to the 'Moderate'. It is worth noting that the other four from the county fell into the latter category.[75]

The Instrument of Government which set up the Protectorate in December 1653 embodied a reform of Parliament limiting its total membership to 400 and reducing Boston's representation from two members to one.[76] In the election for the 1654 Parliament it left the Corporation unsure of how to proceed, as its Minutes show that it spent 30s. on sending someone to London for advice on the matter. It ultimately chose its Recorder, William Ellis. He had sat jointly with Irby in the Long Parliament and was sufficiently favoured by the Army to be allowed to go on sitting in the Rump after Irby's seclusion. With Ellis the Corporation was assured of a voice close to the ear of authority as he was shortly after appointed Solicitor-General by Cromwell.[77]

In the next parliament (1656) Ellis saw fit to sit for Grantham, so Boston returned Irby again; a wasted exercise for he still remained unacceptable to those in power. Appearing at Westminster he was, along with seven other Lincolnshire M.Ps. – half of the county's representation – prevented from sitting by Cromwell's troops. He appealed to the House which in due course advised him to seek satisfaction elsewhere while it got on with the 'great Affairs of the Nation'.[78]

Though the government couldn't pin anything on Irby it clearly suspected him of working against its interest and much of the distrust probably centred upon his connection with Sir William Waller, a one-time Parliamentary General of note but since 1647 detested by the Army and Independent politicians as Presbyterian 'Grandee'. He was sympathetic to the principle of monarchy and several times detained or imprisoned for real or supposed seditious activities. His wife, Anna Paget, was sister to Catherine, Irby's fourth (and last) wife. Irby apparently enjoyed the somewhat hazardous company of his relative, who was also not unknown in Boston. During the mayoral year of 1656-7 the Corporation entertained Sir William at the Peacock Inn, and in 1657-8 he was resident in Irby's London home, the cause of its being searched by government agents for incriminating documents.[79]

It was not until the following Parliament, convened in January 1659, that Irby was able to take his seat unhindered. Cromwell was by then dead and his son, Richard, ruled as Protector. The old form of representation having been reverted to, Irby found himself partnered for Boston with its Deputy Recorder, Francis Mussenden.[80]

The Parliament's task was to find a means of paying off massively accumulated national debts, but instead of legislating it preferred, like its two predecessors, to wrangle over the legality of Protectoral government. Meanwhile the Army looked on in fuming impatience.

Richard lacked the iron-fisted control over the Army which his father had displayed, and its ambitious intriguing generals soon made him close down the Westminster talking-shop. The financial mess however remained, and he next hit upon the idea of recalling the Rump. For Boston this of course brought back Ellis, and later Irby crept in to join him.[81]

The generals' inability to keep their noses out of politics was to ensure that this assembly was to be no more fruitful than the others, and its problems were increased when the Royalists chose this promising-looking time of high discontent to bring to the boil the fourth of their designs referred to earlier. An armed rising, led by a Presbyterian, Sir George Booth, which took place in the West Midlands was quickly put down by forces under Lambert, but throughout July-August 1659 the whole country was in a turmoil of alarm.

In Lincolnshire the militia commissioners were ordered by the Council of State (of which Vane, in the twists and turns of politics, was once again a member) to detain all persons found in arms against the Parliament, while horse races, being convenient rallying points for rebels, were banned. Militia units were brought to readiness, the Holland division and Belvoir Castle rendered secure, and fortifications remaining at Crowland from the 1642 conflict demolished.

Special instructions addressed to Captain Richard Cust ordered him to take charge of arms stored at Lincoln and obtain others from Hull for distribution to the well-affected. Additionally he was to see that taxation money and prisoners accumulated in the city were sent to London under guard. Having also seized a chest of arms at Gainsborough he was directed to secure either the parole or the person of the occupant of nearby Knaith Hall, Lord Willoughby of Parham. As a Parliamentarian, Willoughby had played a big part in Lincolnshire affairs during the Civil War, and had been well known in Boston, but in 1647 he had joined the Royalists and had since been deeply implicated in all of their plots.[82]

Royalist hopes for Boston are revealed in the correspondence of Gervase Holles, the noted antiquarian and soldier. As M.P. for Grimsby he had quit the Parliament at the outbreak of the Civil War to fight for the King, and by 1649, reduced to poverty but remaining fiercely loyal, he had joined Charles II in exile, becoming one of his advisers. As such he drew up a list of Lincolnshire gentry who would be useful in promoting an uprising, and included Irby in it among Presbyterians 'who have heretofore disserved His Majestie, and praetend now to be better disposed either out of a sense of what they have done ill or hatred for the now governing faction'.[83]

In 1658 Holles was nominated to return to Lincolnshire as a secret agent. In letters briefing him, Sir Edward Hyde, Charles's Lord Chancellor, stressed that 'his Majesty wishes that you could possesse yourselfe of Boston', and later warned him that if he should find that against expectations all was quiet, 'and that nothing is prepared at Boston, in God's name then proceed as you shall thinke fitt, and lett not our friends ther looke on whilst the rebells apply all ther power to supresse ther neighbours'. Holles however begged off from the mission on the grounds that lacking funds he could not honourably depart leaving his landlady's bill unpaid. Writing to another Royalist in June 1659 Hyde still thought that Boston 'might be easily possessed', but his optimism was misplaced. The possibility had also occurred to the Council of State who saw to it that 'for better preservation of the peace' the town was garrisoned by companies from the foot regiments of Colonels Sir Bryce Cochrane and Samuel Clarke, recently withdrawn from service in Flanders.[84]

England was then in a state of near-anarchy. After bringing back the Rump Richard Cromwell had resigned the Protectorship, and when the tide of Royalist insurgence ebbed the breach between the Army and Parliament became complete as the latter began to take to itself the business of dispensing and revoking army commissions. Lambert, an Oliver in embryo, prevented it from sitting between October and December 1659, but his support was precarious for his men were heavily in arrears of pay and mutinous. National feeling turned irresistibly toward the only possible solution to the crisis, and when General George Monck, the commander of loyal and tightly disciplined forces stationed in Scotland, declared for a free Parliament and began to march south the Restoration of the King became inevitable.

III. THE RESTORATION

On 16 March 1660 the Long Parliament, which had first met in 1640 and had suffered so many vicissitudes, was finally dissolved. Another was immediately called, and it met on April 25. Boston's representatives were Sir Anthony Irby and Colonel Thomas Hatcher, while sitting for Grimsby was Colonel Edward King. Hatcher had been military governor of Boston from August 1644 to April 1645, having in that post displaced King, who had been unpopular in the town owing to his rigid Presbyterianism and autocratic behaviour. All three individuals were highly active in the affairs of the House, and King is traditionally credited with being the first member to propose reinstating the monarchy.[85]

Charles was formally invited to return on May 1, and he landed from Holland on the 25th. The news of his recall was greeted with general jubilation, causing a Lincolnshire correspondent to write that 'our rough youths make their bones sore with Ringing', and that at Boston they had pulled down the Commonwealth coat of arms, dragged it around the town and flogged it at the whipping post. The tormented object was then urinated upon and consigned to a bonfire.

It was also mayor-making time in Boston. The mayor-elect was Alderman Thomas Welby, a leading local activist for the Parliament in the late wars when, as a sequestration commissioner, he may have used his office to line his own pocket. Undergoing a sudden attack of rectitude he now refused to allow the Corporation Mace to be carried before him until its Commonwealth escutcheon was replaced by the Royal Arms.[86] As will appear, his legal nicety was to avail him little when the crunch came.

The Parliament was dissolved in December, having mainly busied itself with measures for putting the Carriage of State back on its constitutional rails. It also found time vindictively to hound several of the surviving regicides to the scaffold, and almost its last act was to order that Cromwell's corpse be disinterred from Westminster Abbey and hung upon Tyburn gibbet.

Another Parliament was called for 8 May 1661, and an election was held at Boston on April 9. Irby was returned again, this time teamed with Robert Bertie, Lord Willoughby de Eresby. The Corporation, undoubtedly thinking to trim its sails to a coming storm, had invited the latter to stand a week earlier.[87]

He came from a family of ultra-Royalists. His grandfather and Christian namesake, the first Earl of Lindsey, was High Steward of Boston from 1634[88] (a time which coincided with John Cotton's departure from

Boston and government attempts to divert the borough from Puritanism) until 1642 when he was killed fighting for the King at Edgehill. His father, Montagu, current High Steward of Boston,[89] had commanded the Royal Guards at the same battle, and, as already mentioned, had later been obliged to sell Belleau to Sir Henry Vane in compounding for his estates. Robert's uncle, Peregrine, had also commanded a regiment for the King.

On April 18 however a second election took place with Thomas Thory contesting against Irby.[90] Thory's grandfather had been Mayor of Boston in 1566 and his father likewise in 1616 and 1630. In 1642 and 'for divers years before', Thomas, a Cambridge graduate, had been one of Boston's customs collectors. On October 7 of that year he was ordered to join the King at Shrewsbury, where he was appointed one of Charles's personal troop of horse. He was then employed on various duties in the privy chamber until the end of the war. From London on 29 August 1649 he contacted Charles II's secretary, Sir Robert Long, asking him to procure him a place in the King's guard because the Parliament had taken away his estate and he therefore had resolved to live and die with the King. He apparently obtained a post, rising in it to the rank of Major. About July 1660 he petitioned Charles, begging reinstatement as customs collector at Boston, whence he had been ejected during his long absence. His wish was granted but it brought him much trouble, for in 1665 we find him again petitioning, this time for stay of prosecution and pardon of a £1,600 debt which he owed to the Crown from his office. He had used

Fig. 6. CUSTOMS HOUSE, Packhouse Quay, Boston. The building dates from 1725 and occupies the site of a house used for the same purpose from about 1662. Prior to that the customs office stood in the vicinity of the present Grammar School.

the money to pay off creditors who were threatening him with prison. The upshot does not appear.[91]

In the election he and Bertie were returned, and the problem of the double return was referred to a Commons committee for adjudication. Meanwhile, Irby was directed to take the seat. After a two year delay and having its memory jogged by a petition from Thory, the committee found in Irby's favour. The former's claim was declared void, because in its view Boston's inhabitants 'if they were not Freemen, had not voices in the Election,'[92]

It should be made clear that parliamentary representation at this period was still at a stage where M.P.s for cities and boroughs were generally elected by at most a small body of freemen, and frequently (as at Boston) by the members of the Corporation alone. Thory's case was typical of several that arose during the Stuart Parliaments disputing such restriction of the franchise. Boston was also concerned in an earlier example in 1628 when the town clerk led a deputation to London to defend the Corporation's practice. Richard Bellingham the borough's Recorder and Richard Oakely had been elected, but Sir Anthony Irby with 'a Majority of Voices of the Commonalty and Fourteen of the select Number' was challenging the latter. In the decision rendered Oakely was ousted and the opinion given that elections 'in all boroughs, did, of common right, belong to the commoners; and that nothing could take it from them but a prescription and a constant use beyond all memory'.[93] This fine libertarian sentiment, flawed though it is by its closing acknowledgement of the status quo through established precedent, reflected accurately the temper of the Parliament of 1628, which was responsible for the Petition of Right. After it, Charles I imposed his so-called 'Eleven Years' Tyranny' that was to be soon followed by the Civil War. The wording of an entry in Boston's Corporation Minutes of the election of members for the next, the 'Short Parliament' of 1640, shows that the Mayor and Burgesses were not overawed by the 1628 decision, and carried on as of old.[94]

From a reading of the Thory judgement it may be inferred that since 1640 some improvement had been effected whereby all of Boston's freemen were permitted to vote, but the reality was less comprehensive. Worth noting is a similar decision handed down in 1661 for another Lincolnshire borough, Stamford, whose wording is more exact. There the question was whether 'every Freeman of the said Borough, or only such Freemen as paid Scot and Lot, had Right of Election: And that, upon the Evidence, it appeared, That such Freemen only, as paid Scot and Lot, had Right of Election'. Further Boston election rulings made by the Commons in the early eighteenth century indicate that this type of qualification was also applied in Boston.[95] The payment referred to was a tax which Corporations levied upon their members to defray administrative expenses.

Even if all of Boston's freemen had held voting rights, the democratic position would still have been a far cry from that pertaining today. A rough appreciation of how far can be arrived at from an examination of

23

the surviving Freemans' Admission Book[96] which shows a total of 700 admissions taking place between 1600 and mid 1661. Allowing for wastage over this period by death and other reasons it can be guessed that in the latter year the freemen in the borough might have numbered in the region of 400. If, further, a likely figure of around 2,500 is accepted as the population at this time, with 900 of this total discounted as minors, then it can be estimated that the freemen could not have amounted to more than about a quarter of the adult community.[97]

The Parliament of 1661 lasted until 1679, but Bertie left Irby's side in 1666 on succeeding to the Earldom of Lindsey and being elevated to the Lords. He became High Steward of Boston in the same year.[98] His place was filled by Sir Philip Harcourt, of Stanton Harcourt, Oxfordshire, who perhaps had to stand for the seat against Sir Edward Barkham, of Wainfleet, whose aunt was Irby's third wife.[99] Even so, the choice of Harcourt still meant that Boston's representation was a cosy family affair. His wife was daughter by the second marriage of Sir William Waller. Her aunt by her father's third marriage was Irby's fourth wife. Waller's third wife was Sir Philip's widowed mother. Harcourt's only mark in the annals of the Commons seems to have been made in 1677 when his outstretched leg sent Andrew Marvell, the famous poet and satirist and M.P. for Hull, sprawling. In return Marvell boxed Harcourt's ears, and although both men later claimed that it was only friendly horseplay it was taken as an affront to the dignity of the House and there was talk of committal to the Tower before it all subsided.[100]

Whereas the 1660 Parliament had been composed of a mixture of King's men and erstwhile Parliamentarians of the Irby cast, that of 1661 was so virulently Royalist as to earn the nickname of the Cavalier Parliament. It was therefore a willing legislative machine for realising the government's plans for dominating the Municipalities and re-establishing the Church as its propaganda and indoctrination apparatus.

The first objective was attained through the 1661 Act for the well-Governing and Regulating of Corporations, which required all members of such to take the sacraments of the Church of England, oaths of allegiance and non-resistance to the King, and repudiate the Solemn League and Covenant. For each corporation five commissioners were nominated, who until 25 March 1663 had full power to purge and appoint as they saw fit. The five selected for Boston were Sir Anthony Oldfield, Sir John Walpole, Philip Tyrwhit, Francis Wingfield, and Thomas Thory, the borough's putative M.P.

Most of the Corporation would have known instantly that they could expect little flexibility from this group. The first three were all Lincolnshire men. Oldfield, recently created baronet, hailed from Spalding. His father had been severely wounded in the King's service at the siege of Newark, and had to redeem his estate against a fine of £1,390 imposed by the Parliament. In 1645, while under sequestration, the estate (and Sir Anthony's inheritance) had been put at the disposal of the Boston Corporation, which was allowed to milk it to the tune of £2,000. Sir

Anthony had already tried, unsuccessfully, to have Colonel Edmund Syler, a leading Bostonian, exempted from the Act of Oblivion.[101] Sir John Walpole of Dunston, Standard Bearer to both Charles I and II, had surrendered with the garrison of Oxford and had also compounded for his estate.[102] Philip Tyrwhit, of Stainfield, was soon to succeed to his father's baronetcy. His father was currently High Sheriff of Lincolnshire (an office passed to Oldfield in 1662) and had been a heavily committed Royalist. Custodian of the county magazine in 1642 he had taken up arms and had his home plundered during the war. Afterwards he sustained a crippling fine of nearly £3,500 to retain his estate.[103] Wingfield will be dealt with shortly.

The axe did not fall upon the Corporation until 2 September 1662. The heraldry-conscious Thomas Welby and seven of his companions, being three-quarters of the aldermanic body, were then dismissed and supplanted by the commission's place-men, three of whom were up-graded common councillors. Eight, almost half of the common councillors, were likewise sacked and replaced. One of the two Sergeants-at-Mace was removed and the other resigned. James Preston, the sitting Mayor, was ejected and his office given to George Slee, the port's customs controller. All of the new Corporation took the required oaths except two of the common councillors, who were not present.[104]

Ironically, during the previous year, before the passing of the Corporations Act, the King had contrived to get an Act through the Parliament allowing him to pass the hat around the country for a 'Free and Voluntary Gift' of money to himself. A meeting at Boston had considered it on September 20, almost exactly a year before the ejections, and among the subscribers may be found the names of all the expelled aldermen, contributing sums of up to £5. Looking back, they must now have ruefully sighed over the poor return for their investment.[105]

George Slee, the new mayor, was a long-time resident of Boston who had originally sprung from Barnstaple in Devon.[106] His son, Andrew, one of the new aldermen, was to be mayor in 1664 and 1675. Set against his family background, George Slee's mayoralty can be seen as a link bringing full circle to a period of almost fifty years of Boston's politico-religious history. His wife was the daughter of Andrew Baron, who had preceded him as the port's customs controller. Baron's elder brother, Peter,[107] practised medicine in Boston until his death in 1630. They were of a French emigré family, and their father, also named Peter, was a noted theologian who had been befriended by Lord Burghley, through whose influence he had been appointed Lady Margaret Professor of Divinity in the University of Cambridge. Once installed he caused much controversy by his espousal of Arminianism, a moderate theology that ran counter to the prevailing trend towards Puritanism. Peter, the son, arrived in Boston sometime before 1606[108] and seems to have been of an assertive nature. By 1609 he was on the Corporation and had made sufficient enemies within it to get embroiled in a row over his position in the aldermanic pecking order. He appealed to the borough's Recorder,

Thomas Cecil, Earl of Exeter, the now deceased Burghley's son, and his influence with him seems to have been greater than the Corporation's. Exeter sent his 'loving friends' a slightly menacing letter favouring Baron, whom the Corporation, sooner than offend their powerful patron, then duly accommodated. To keep the Earl sweet they sent him a present. Baron became mayor in 1610 and so assiduously disseminated his father's doctrine that in 1612, when John Cotton began his ministry in Boston, he found that many of the leading citizens had been leavened by it. Cotton's teaching and influence prevailed however, and the borough embarked upon the Puritan road that it was to follow right through the Civil War and Interregnum.[109]

A major Corporation office which the commissioners did not need to take under scrutiny was that of the Recorder. Ellis, with his history of service to the Protectorate, did not wait for the inevitable but submitted his resignation by letter a month before the commission sat. He was a surviving type and lived to receive a knighthood from Charles and become a Justice of the Common Pleas. In the Parliament of 1679 he was returned once again for Boston but sat only technically, standing down after twenty-six days to make way for Sir William Yorke.[110]

The vacancy he created was filled by the Attorney General, Sir Geoffrey Palmer, of Carlton, Northants, M.P. for Ludgershall, Wilts. He had been an original member of the Long Parliament, representing Stamford, Lincs., but in 1642 he had left the House for the Royalist Parliament at Oxford, an act of loyalty that cost him a £500 compounding fine in 1648. One of his daughters married into the de la Fountaine family of Kirby Belers, Leicestershire, and this linked him into the families of Baron, Slee, and Tyrwhit.[111] Like most of Boston's Recorders he must have been seen only rarely in the town, and his choice of deputy fell upon a distant cousin, Francis Wingfield, the fifth of Boston's 'regulators' as yet unconsidered.[112]

Wingfield derived from Tickencote in Rutlandshire. He was related to Sir Geoffrey through his first wife, a Palmer of Stoke Doyle, which was a cadet branch of the Carlton family. In 1660 he had been M.P. for Stamford, having disputed the seat with a Republican John Weaver, who in the 'recruiter elections' of 1645 had cornered the seat abandoned by Palmer. Wingfield's aunt was wife to the uncle of Sir Anthony Oldfield, while his sister-in-law was the daughter of royalist Sir William Thorold, the present M.P. for Grantham. Further afield, his great-aunt, Dorothy Wingfield, was the wife of Adam Claypole of Northborough, whose grandson, John, was son-in-law to Oliver Cromwell.[113] Francis Wingfield remained as Deputy Recorder until his death in 1677.

While taming the corporations the government also trained its sights upon the potentially explosive target of religion. The question of what form the Established Church should take had been the subject of long debate in the 1660 Parliament, and although a compromise system combining presbytery and episcopacy was worked out it was not realised before the dissolution.[114] Now, undiluted Anglicanism was reinstated,

26

and under the 1662 Act of Uniformity all of the puritan clergy, many of whom had during the previous twenty years been installed in livings at the expense of their evicted orthodox bretheren, found themselves faced with a crisis of conscience. They were given until St. Bartholomew's Day (August 25) 1662 to accept the full rites of the Church of England and take the oaths laid down in the Corporations Act, or suffer ejection.

The Vicar of Boston was Obadiah Howe, late incumbent of Gedney. His father, William, who had been minister of Tattershall, was reputedly a 'grand Presbyterian and Independent' during the Protectorate. Obadiah had been minister of Stickney in 1643 where he is said to have entertained Cromwell and other Parliamentarian officers before the battle of Winceby. Whatever his opinions then, they did not prevent him from conforming now, and he retained the Boston living until his death in 1683. At the ejections he had been vicar for only two years. His predecessor, Anthony Tuckney, was a big fish in the pond of Puritan theology. A cousin to John Cotton, he had entered the living in 1633 upon Cotton's departure for America. From about 1645 however he began to carve out a distinguished academic career for himself and became a shepherd *in absentia*, leaving his flock to a curate, Bankes Anderson, who was joined in his labours from 1648 onwards by another cleric, John Naylor. On 8 April 1659 the Corporation asked Tuckney, perhaps because of his continual absence, to resign the vicarate. In August 1660 it was obliged to ask him again, this time sending him a form of presentation and inviting him to write in his successor, but voting to appoint Howe regardless if no response was forthcoming – which apparently it was not. Tuckney was in due course also politely deprived of his University posts by the authorities. The fate of John Naylor is obscure. Bankes Anderson refused to conform and was cast out into the wilderness.[115]

The clergy and laity who would not compromise with their principles – the hard core of the 'Puritans' of yesteryear – now achieved a new identity as Nonconformists, or Dissenters, and for the most part found a spiritual home in Presbyterian or Baptist congregations. Not until the Toleration Act of 1689 however did these obtain enduring legal sanction and a foothold in social respectability, and meanwhile their members had to submit to suppression and persecution. In 1664 the provisions of the Act of Uniformity were reinforced by those of the Conventicles Act, which equated illegal prayer meetings with plotters' councils, and a year later came the Five Mile Act which prohibited all nonconforming clergy from residing or coming within that distance of any place where they had formerly held livings.

Walter Wilson, the historian of Nonconformity, was of the opinion that a Presbyterian congregation was formed in Boston shortly after the the ejections, and infers that Bankes Anderson, who died in 1668, was its founder. There is no proof of this.[116] Authentic information does not become available until 1672 when the King promulgated the Declaration of Indulgence. This extended tolerance to Catholics and Dissenters alike and was born out of the cynical wheelings and dealings that attended the conclusion of the Treaty of Dover between England and France. Parliament opposition forced Charles to withdraw it a year later, but while it flourished dwellings throughout the country became licensed for religious meetings. In Boston the house of William Cooper was licensed for Presbyterian worship on 9 December 1672, and the congregation adopted Thomas Spademan, 'much esteem'd for his Learning, Diligence, and Charity', as its pastor. Before being ejected in 1662 he had been rector of Althorpe in the Isle of Axholme, where his peaceable demeanour was such that afterwards the authorities allowed him to continue in residence, unmolested. He died at Boston in 1678.[117]

The borough already had a Baptist community dating back at least as early as 1653, when its pastors were Richard Craford and Edward Cock. During that year Thomas Grantham, a native of Halton, near Spilsby, was baptized into the faith at Boston. He was ordained pastor, either at Boston or Halton, three years later and went on to attain considerable eminence in the Baptist movement. He was present at a conventicle in Boston in 1662 when troops broke it up and carried him off to Lincoln Goal, an event that set a pattern of agitation and persecution which was to characterise a good deal of his subsequent career. At the Indulgence, on 28 October 1672, the Boston house of John Ashwell was licensed for Baptist worship.[118]

The official responsible for implementing the edicts against Nonconformists in Lincolnshire was Sir Edward Lake, its Diocesan Chancellor. He had received the appointment, below his deserts, for services to the throne that involved being wounded sixteen times in battle. He provides another example of how royalist Boston's complexion had become, for on 10 October 1662 he was appointed Judge of its Admiralty Court,[119] and remained so until his death in 1674. As Chancellor he was no vindictive persecutor, though he might well have been, considering the provocation he sustained and the gout from which he suffered. Colonel Edward King, then the stormy petrel of Lincolnshire politics, is said to have set on ninety law suits against him on behalf of Nonconformists, four of which having been brought to trial, King was cast in all of them. In a letter to the Secretary of the Council of State, Sir Edward groaned his hope that 'we may not be trod down by this malicious generation of men'.[120] Curiously enough, this deeply loyal old cavalier had strong Puritan shadings in his family background. His father-in-law, Simon Bibye, may have been the same person as, or a relative of, an individual of that name who is said to have been charmed by the Corporation into being instrumental in obtaining the vicarage of Boston for John Cotton in 1612. Lake's step-brother, Thomas, emigrated to Boston, Massachusetts, about 1648, where he married the daughter of Stephen Goodyear, deputy governor of New Haven Colony from 1641 to 1650. Their daughter married twice, firstly to John Cotton's grandson, and secondly to Increase Mather, whose father had married Cotton's widow.[121]

IV. THE SECOND DUTCH WAR

While these domestic convulsions had been taking place England's relations with the Dutch Republic had been steadily worsening as the mercantile and empire-building aspirations of the two countries came into conflict again.

The Dutch declared war in December 1664 and the effect was quickly felt by the sea-going fraternity. About that time we find Matthew Burchenall, master of the *Providence* of Boston, lying in the Thames, petitioning with other masters for a convoy and that some of their press-ganged men should be returned, as they considered it risky to sail with makeshift crews of aged and foreign seamen.[122]

There were fears that the war would afford opportunities for political malcontents to foment mischief, and the Boston region had its share of rumours. Sixty of 'Oliver's old boys' were said to have mustered at Ely, promising themselves 'that they should have a day soon,' while a conventicle of several hundred, including 'many of quality from Rutlandshire' was prevented from being held at Castle Bytham. The Dutch were believed to have formed two regiments of Roundhead fugitives, and Anthony Oldfield, writing from Spalding to a friend in London, described a conversation with a Lynn merchant come from Dordrecht who had there seen the regicide, Colonel Valentine Walton, late military governor of Lynn, 'disguised in a periwig down to his waist'. A Dutchman threatened the merchant 'to knock his brains out if he did anything concerning Walton, finding that he knew him'.[123]

The effects of the war on Boston are unknown until the middle of 1666 when the letters of Robert Gray, an 'honest man' of the town who was engaged by the Clerk of the Post Office to report intelligence, become available.

They show that July of that year was a hectic month for Boston and its mariners. The town was busy raising volunteers, while Dutch privateers, aided by others from France which had now entered the war against England, were cruising along the Lincolnshire coast and into the Wash. One took two Boston ships and fired a third, and although the town promptly sent out a vessel manned by fifty men to hunt down the culprit, he could not be found. Shortly after, a collier was chased into the port by a French sloop that had also run three others ashore at Wainfleet, where the local inhabitants came to their rescue. The Boston collier *Thomas and John* was not so lucky. Hove to in Grimsby Roads it was captured by a cutting out party sent into the Humber from a Dutch ship. The master, Thomas Chaplin, managed to escape with his crew. Grimsby seamen witnessed the incident but were unable to intervene owing to adverse tidal conditions.[124]

Gray opined that the coast needed the protection of a man-of-war, but the Navy had its hands full, and only a month earlier it had been severely mauled in the so-called Four Days' Battle off the Kent coast. A glimpse of how grim a seaman's life generally could be in this age is afforded through a letter of John Tellford, master of the London ship *Charles;* written in September 1666 which was a month of violent gales. In putting six men ashore at Hull he feared that they were in such a sad state that their hands would have to be amputated.[125]

On July 25, Gray reported that cannonading had been heard in the town, coming from the south-east. Also, a French sloop, perhaps the one referred to earlier, had closed a ship standing into the Boston Deeps and received a nasty surprise. The ship was the *Truelove*, a navy frigate that was collecting volunteers and pressed men for transmission to the Fleet. When its gun-ports crashed open the Frenchman took advantage of his shallower draught to beat off for safety beyond the Longsand. In Boston the frigate was victualled on credit by Alderman Andrew Slee. Five months later Sir Anthony Irby was obliged to remind the Navy Commissioners to honour the debt.[126]

In August the Earl of Lindsey's troop of horse lay at Boston before marching for Lynn. It was probably employed in scouting the coast for enemy landing parties or guarding against internal unrest. After the war it was disbanded at Boston and delivered its arms and equipment to the Mayor for safe-keeping.[127]

In October Gray had nothing to report save that the town was in good health; no casual remark for the Midlands and South-East England were then in the grip of bubonic plague. Having ravaged London in 1665 with results that are well known, the infection, probably ship-borne, spread into the coastal towns and continued to effect them throughout 1666. By some freak Lincolnshire was spared,[128] but the disease prowled around its southern flanks, invading Peterborough and Cambridge. At Newark one third of the inhabitants are said to have died and grass grew in the streets. Lynn had some deaths but staved off worse mortality with a strict quarantine.[129]

Boston would probably have suffered if the Corporation had not taken the precaution, in 1665, of cancelling the Great Mart which began annually on St. Andrew's Day (Nov. 30) and to which there was 'greate resorts from London and many places in the realme'. It had adopted this tactic once before during an outbreak in 1603 when to secure its legal position it had first obtained the King's sanction for the move. A similar course was now taken, and its intention was broadcast on 10 November 1665 through a Royal Proclamation issued by Charles from his Court at Oxford.[130]

The Corporation's intermediary in this business was Sir Robert Carr of Sleaford, a *bon viveur* and horse-racing crony of the King. He was also

BY THE KING

A PROCLAMATION

Prohibiting the keeping of the Mart at BOSTON, *in the County of* LINCOLN.

CHARLES REX,.

THe Kings moſt Excellent Majeſty, out of His Princely and Chriſtian care of his loving Subjects, That no good means of Providence may be neglected, to ſtay the further ſpreading of the great Infection of the Plague, doth finde it neceſſary to prevent all occaſions of Publick Concourſe of His People for the preſent, till it ſhall pleaſe Almighty God, of His Goodneſs, to ceaſe the violence of the Contagion, which is very far diſperſed into many parts of this Kingdom already; and therefore, remembring that there is at hand a Mart or Fair of Note, unto which there is uſually extraordinary Reſort out of ſeveral Parts of the Kingdom, kept at *Boſton* in the County of *Lincoln*; The holding whereof at the uſual time, would, in all likelyhood, be the occaſion of further Danger and Infection to other Parts of the Land, which yet, by Gods Mercy, ſtands clear and free, Hath (with the Advice of his Privy Councel) thought good, by this open Declaration of his Pleaſure and neceſſary Commandment, not onely to admoniſh and require all his loving Subjects to forbear to Reſort, for this time, to the ſaid Mart or Fair kept at *Boſton* aforeſaid, or to any other Fair or Fairs in the ſaid County of *Lincoln*; But alſo to enjoyn the Lord or Lords of the ſaid Fair, or others intereſted therein, that they all forbear to hold the ſaid Fair, or any thing appertaining thereunto, at the time accuſtomed, or at any other time, till by Gods goodneſs and mercy the Infection of the Plague ſhall ceaſe, or be ſo much diminiſhed, that His Majeſty ſhall give Order for holding them, upon pain of ſuch Puniſhment, as for a Contempt, ſo much concerning the general Safety of His People, they ſhall be adjudged to deſerve, which they muſt expect to be Inflicted with all ſeverity. And to that purpoſe, doth hereby further charge and enjoyn (under the like Penalty) all Citizens and Inhabitants of the Cities of *London* and *Weſtminſter*, That none of them ſhall repair unto any Fairs, held within any part of this Kingdom, until it ſhall pleaſe God to ceaſe the Infection ſtill continuing amongſt them. His Majeſties Intention being, and ſo hereby Declaring Himſelf, That no Lord of any Fair, or others intereſted in the Profits thereof, ſhall, by this neceſſary and temporary Reſtraint, receive any prejudice in the right of his or their Fairs, or Liberties thereunto belonging; any thing before-mentioned notwithſtanding. *Given at Our Court at* Oxford, *the Tenth Day of* November, *in the Seventeenth Tear of our Reign.*

GOD SAVE THE KING.

OXFORD,

Printed by *Leonard Lichfield*, Printer to the Univerſity, For *John Bill*, and *Chriſtopher Barker*, Printers to the KING'S moſt Excellent Majeſty. *Anno Dom.* 1665.

Fig. 7.   Royal Proclamation, 10 November 1665, forbidding the holding of Boston Mart in order to prevent the spreading of Plague. (Public Record Office: SP 45/11).

an energetic Deputy-Lieutenant and M.P. for Lincolnshire, later becoming Chancellor of the Duchy of Lancaster, 'a honourable place, worth £1,200 per annum, and admitting of much ease and quiet'. His wife was sister to the Earl of Arlington, a member of the infamous 'Cabal' administration. Carr also appears to have been connected to the Baron family.

In March 1666 the Corporation voted him a present of £5 value in appreciation of his help. He acknowledged it as being at all times willing to be of service, and in 1670 when Sir Geoffrey Palmer died, he was taken up on this. At that time the Corporation, which had presumably come to enjoy the convenience of having the Attorney General as its Recorder, first offered the vacancy to the new holder of that office, Sir Heneage Finch. He turned it down however and it was then offered to Carr, who accepted. Modern practice requires a Recorder to be a qualified barrister of a minimum of five years standing, but the laxity of Carr's day was such that when appointed he was not even a barrister! Over a year later he condescended to obtain entry to Gray's Inn, and after a mere three months was called to the Bar *ex gratia*.[131]

Notwithstanding his lack of qualifications, his letters show that he was diligent in caring for the town's interests, which probably coincided with his own. In 1671 he managed to get both himself and Boston into serious trouble concerning customs regulations. Although the details are cloudy it appears that he illegally licensed the town's brewers to lend out their brewing vessels, thereby infringing the Customs Act of 1663 (15 Car. II, c.xi). The business seems eventually to have been smoothed over, but during the course of it he was obliged to stress in his defence that Boston was the only port Lincolnshire had, and that its destruction would be prejudicial to the whole county.[132]

The Dutch War dragged on into its third year, and with the passing of the winter gales corsairs again appeared in the Wash. The Newcastle coal trade was completely disrupted. Gray noted that three colliers were captured near Freiston and that the price of coal in the town was extraordinarily high.[133]

The ordeal ended when peace was concluded at Breda on 31 July 1667. The Navy had held the edge until the very last when, owing to lack of finance to keep them operational, its ships were decommissioned and laid up in the Medway. There the Dutch boldly forced an entry and put them to the torch, inflicting a humiliating defeat whose memory became fertile ground for the growth of yet another Anglo-Dutch conflict.

During the war seamen had been paid irregularly, and promissory notes had been issued for redemption at a later date. Bearing upon this the town crier went around Boston in 1668, advising all who had any outstanding claim or complaint to present themselves to the magistrates, and a crop of pathetic depositions resulted.

Alexander Thompson told how in 1664 he was pressed out of the *John and Thomas* of Boston at Ousely Bay into *HMS Mermaid* where he had served for two years. He had lost a leg in action and had received no pay whatsoever. Richard Burdall, pressed out of the same ship into the *Coast* frigate had died on active service and his father claimed on his behalf. Matthew Wilson, taken out of the *William* of Boston at Queenborough on the Isle of Sheppey into the frigate *Portland*, had been wounded and had 'continued sickly ever since', but had received only four out of eighteen months pay due. Thomas Rutland, the master of the *William*, reported that at Rye in 1664 he had lost his apprentice, James Asquit, into the *Mary* frigate. Fourteen months later Asquit was travelling home on leave to Boston by sea when the *Francis and John*, in which he had taken passage, was captured by a Dutch warship and he was taken prisoner to Holland. It was still unknown whether he was alive or dead. William Kippis and Richard Clayton, mariners of Boston, also claimed compensation for their time as prisoners of war. Susanna Mould entered a claim for her son, Thomas, slain while under the command of Rear Admiral Sir John Harman, probably in the great Four Days' Battle of June 1666. The blow was doubly hard for she was a widow. Her late husband was Captain Edward Mould, who it will be recalled was master of the protection vessel *Concord* in 1653.[134]

Another footnote to the struggle, indicative of the damage it caused to the port's shipping resources, appears in an order issued in March 1671, permitting the naturalisation of a prize vessel purchased by 'certain of Boston, who had lost most of their own in the late war'.[135]

Fig. 8.

- Ketch -

V. THE THIRD DUTCH WAR

After the war Boston's seamen enjoyed five years of peace, punctuated only by their accepted occupational hazards, as in 1668 when the *Lamb* perished on a voyage to Rotterdam, and in 1671 when a ketch belonging to the port was lost with all hands off Yarmouth during a storm.[136]

During this period, due to the Medway disaster and his history of dissolute extravagance, Charles's popularity and that of his government sharply declined. To shore up his depleted finances he concluded the Treaty of Dover which allied England to France for a new war against the Dutch. While Louis XIV's troops were to invade the Low Countries, the English Navy was to destroy the Dutch fleet. In return for this and a secret commitment to restore England to the Catholic faith, Charles was to receive a large cash subsidy and certain Dutch coastal territory.

Hostilities began in March 1672. Sir Robert Carr reported to the Secretary of the Council of State that Lincolnshire was 'in very good temper and well persuaded of the war' and that Boston's newly chosen Mayor, John Boult, was 'highly loyal'. For his part, Jonathan Smith, collector of customs, nervously took note that the port was 'small and likely to be very perilous' and prayed that 'Jehovah grant salvation to be bulwarks about us'. At this time the *Blessing* of Boston seems to have narrowly escaped being the port's first casualty when it stopped in the English Channel to supply a large homeward-bound Dutch ship with provisions. Both were apparently unaware that war had been declared.[137]

Once again our knowledge of Boston's involvement is due to detailed correspondence surviving among the State Papers; being that of Colonel John Butler who appears to have become Chief Customs Officer, or Controller, of Boston about 1670, vice George Slee. Of his antecedents nothing can be discovered, but he may have been related to Anthony Butler who was promoted from Common Councillor to Alderman in the Corporation purge of 1662 and became Mayor in 1667.[138]

Colonel Butler was a highly conscientious officer. In the first weeks of the war he cruised the Wash regularly in the custom-house vessel seeking intelligence on enemy shipping, and gave his opinion that the Dutch would issue no letters of marque to privateers until they had first creamed off their best seamen into their main battle fleet.

On the 2 and 3 May the press gang was busy in Boston and a total of 'forty choice seamen' was set marching for Hull, where, together with others from Saltfleet and Grimsby, they became something of an unwelcome administrative problem until they were finally sent off to the Fleet.[139]

Trouble began about the end of May when three colliers bound out of Boston for Sunderland were intercepted by a six gun sloop. Two made it into Grainthorpe, but the third was forced ashore and would have been plundered if the coastal inhabitants had not turned out in force and poured small arms fire into the Dutch landing party.

Numerous privateers now appeared, attacking English and foreign merchantmen indiscriminately, so that by June trade had ground to a standstill. Some of the marauders were Scottish, and a particularly active and powerful twenty-gun Dutch ship employed the ruse of concealing its identity by covering its decorated stern with a canvas. One keen-eyed skipper who was taken aboard for interrogation was able to note, however, that its design incorporated two seahorses. Nevertheless a large fleet of eighty southbound colliers was permitted to reach and pass Boston unmolested because many of its number were heavily armed.[140]

A report by Butler at the end of June struck a lighter vein by commenting upon a seventy foot whale stranded at Wrangle, 'which by being a novelty causes many a hundred to go and see her'. Ever watchful of its Admiralty rights, the Corporation soon had it 'boiling near the town, and five or six tun of oil will probably be got out of what is brought hither in pieces, the country people having previously cut and carried off a great quantity of it'.[141]

By July 3, when the war was four months old, Butler was able to state that Boston had not lost a single ship, and that a lull in enemy activity had caused trade to revive and brought down the price of coal. Yet by the end of the month, despite foul weather, the situation had reverted and the coast was 'so infested with small privateers that our merchants dare not send a vessel to sea'. Near Wainfleet and Ingoldmells three colliers delivering cargo were surprised by a small 'picaroon' that captured and made off with two of them. Some of their crew that had escaped joined the third, which was armed, and together with 'twelve stout countrymen' they not only retook the two ships but pursued the Dutchman seven leagues to sea before giving up the chase. Pugnacity seems to have been a characteristic of seventeenth century Lincolnshire coast dwellers. They were certainly not unversed in the rough and tumble of piracy, as barely a hundred years earlier Ingoldmells Haven had enjoyed the unsavoury sobriquet of 'Thieves Creek'.

The vessel so ignominiously put to flight had been cruising the area waiting for the arrival of a Boston wine-ship, the *Happy Entrance*, master William Full, which had been on passage home from Bordeaux since May 1. When it at last hove into sight however the privateer captain was powerless to take it by reason of having already severely depleted his man-power in furnishing crews for his earlier prizes. Butler noted that this was a lucky circumstance for the London insurers of Full's cargo.[142]

Butler writes of the *Happy Entrance* as being Boston's best ship. It was certainly well favoured by the wine cellars of the nobility, as its consignment lading for a voyage made two years earlier reads like Debrett, including the names of four earls and five baronets. Unfortunately it was to fall into the hands of a privateer seven months later through 'venturing without a pilot'.[143]

Throughout August 1672 the pressure was maintained. On the 17th Butler wrote that an inward bound ship of the port had been taken, and that no ship had stirred in or out of Boston for three weeks. Eleven privateers were ranging between the Humber and the Wash, while between Wainfleet and Saltfleet homesteads located near the sea were forced to keep night watch for fear of being raided by parties from small single-gun ships whose shallow draught enabled them to creep so close inshore that 'none dare ride or walk on the sea bank when they see them near'. Captain Anthony Irby, Sir Anthony's son, saw fit to muster a troop of horse at Boston, 'most with buff coats and good horses, to the great satisfaction of the Lord Lieutenant and Deputy Lieutenants present'.[144]

The harbours of both Boston and King's Lynn were soon packed with fugitive vessels, and the mayor and inhabitants of the latter, depressed by the slump in trade, were moved to complain that although the main Newcastle-London shipping lane, eighty miles offshore, received convoy protection, privateers were allowed to operate with impunity between it and the coast.

The Navy Commissioners stirred themselves, and on September 21 two sixth rates, the *Fanfan*, Captain John Pybus, and the *Deptford Ketch*, Captain Edward Anguish, entered the Wash for convoy duty. Both were from the squadron of Sir Edward Spragg, Vice-Admiral of the Red, and Pybus's ship had lately been employed in carrying the corpse of the Earl of Sandwich to London after his death in the Battle of Sole Bay. Two other ships, the *Barnaby* and the *Sweepstakes*, were assigned to the Humber.[145]

TRANSCRIPTION OF LETTER OPPOSITE

Boston the 17 of August 1672

Sr.

the winde is now neare at South a little Easterly: for anything worth your knowledg I have little newe haveing noe trade nowe: lately wee lost a vessell beelonging to this Port laden from Boordeaux: wee have had noe vessell Com into: nor gon out of this Port this 3 weekes but one small Ketch: the Privateers doe soe infest these Partes: that beetween this and the Mouth of Humber wee are told of a 11 saile and that beetweene: Wainfleet and Saltfleete: the marsh men that live neere to the Sea: are forced to joyne together and keepe watch a nightes for feare of beeing Plundered and ruined by these little Capers who sum of them have but one Gun: and draw soe little water that they will Com soe neere the Shore at High water: that non dare ride or walk upon the Sea Banke when: they bee neere: yesterday heare was mustered 2 Companies of traind band foote and Captaine Erbyes troope of Horse: most in Buff Coates: and Good Horses to the great saticefaccon of the Lord leiutenent and deputy Lord leiutennants who weare presant at the Muster: Sr. I am

Your Most Humble

Servant Jo. Butler.

Sr. Since I had written my letter a privateere tooke a Collier and plundered 3 danes and Chased in John Thomson Master of a small vessell from London into the very port: who very hardly scaped thence.

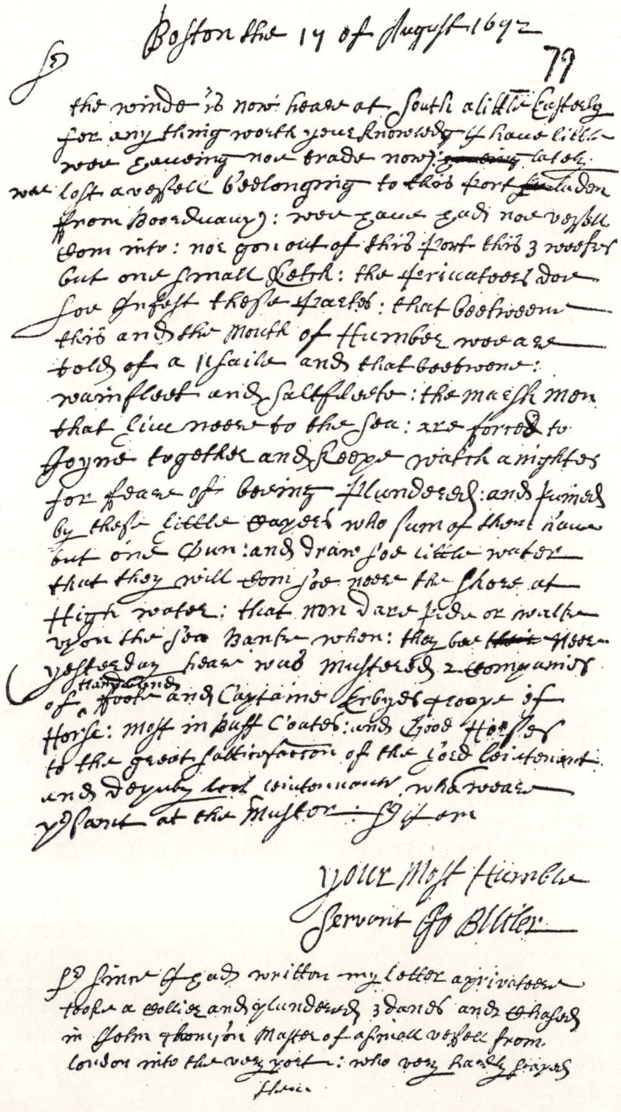

Fig. 9. Letter of Colonel John Butler, Chief Customs Officer of Boston, to Sir Joseph Williamson, Secretary to the Council of State. Public Record Office. SP 29/314. (This letter is reduced to approximately half original size – a transcription appears opposite.)

These vessels appear to have remained on station until at least June of the following year. Afterwards they were either supplanted or supplemented by the *William Dogger*, of eight guns, commanded by a Captain Smith. This ship was procured for Boston's benefit through the 'signal kindnesse' of the Earl of Lindsey and Sir Robert Carr, to whom a grateful Corporation voted a tierce (approx. 40 gallons) of wine apiece. The register of St. Botolph's records the burial of 'Capt. Smith of the convoy' on 9 December 1673, but whether he died of natural causes or by enemy action is not given.[146]

Trade now resumed, and by October 9 Butler records that Boston was plentifully supplied with coal, '20 sail now delivering'. On the night of October 16, Captain John Wood of the *Kent* arrived in Boston with a tale of woe. The day before he had left his ship run aground and breaking up on the Leman Bank, a shoal now much favoured by gas drilling rigs which stands some 75 miles east of Boston. Abandoning 200 men aboard he had embarked with a handful of the crew in the ship's pinnace, eventually making the Lincolnshire coast at Trusthorpe. He begged Butler to send out a vessel in search of survivors. In order to obtain one, Butler, Mayor John Boult, and four other inhabitants had to stand bound in the sum of £80 to its owner against its capture by the enemy. Despatched with provisions and the port's best pilot it cruised for three days without finding any trace of the ship or its crew. It later transpired that in the intervening period the survivors had been rescued from the rapidly disintegrating wreck by a kindly disposed Dutch privateer, the *Geeldseer*, commanded by Captain Adrian Direchst. He intended to put them ashore at Yarmouth under a flag of truce, but on the way there he made the mistake of closing and challenging a 'collier' that turned out to be the *Portsmouth*, a warship that obliged him under threat of its heavier armament to surrender. Later however, the Navy Commissioners extended him the civility of an award of £140 for his life-saving efforts.

Considerable remains of the *Kent* duly washed up on the sands north of Boston, and Butler was much concerned about their recovery and also that of the pinnace left at Trusthorpe, fearing that it would be 'pulled to pieces by the poor people and burnt'. He considered that the ship's loss was due to negligence of its pilot, but in the subsequent enquiry that individual defended himself on the grounds that he had been entrusted merely with taking the ship from Woolwich to the Hope for discharge. Once under way, Wood, who was probably a prize-hungry fanatic, had taken the charge from him 'and like a madman, ran the ship what way his fancy pleased him. If I but advised him to take in the topsails, or we should carry our mast by the board, he answered let the topmast and sail go to the devil'.[147]

The onset of winter brought fresh dangers. A fleet of seventy colliers, thirty from Boston and the remainder from Lynn, left the Wash in late October bound north and ran straight into a violent gale. Butler thought that many would have perished unless they had made the shelter of the Humber on the first night out.[148]

On November 2, the *New Exchange* of Boston was taken by a privateer and then rescued by one of H.M. frigates, while a fortnight later several men from the *Crown*, a fourth rate of 46 guns came into Boston looking for their ship which had dragged from its anchor and vanished while they were ashore at Scarborough. The general effect of the weather was to drive away friend and enemy alike, and on November 20 Boston's custom house vessel put in after cruising the coast for ten days without sighting a single sail. Prospects for the November mart began to look dim, but on the 30th, just in time, Butler was able to write that several ships had arrived under guard from the Thames 'to the great joy of the Londoners who had great concerns in those vessels for this mart'.[149]

The new year brought little cause for celebration to the inhabitants of the Great Level to the south of Boston, for everything they possessed was either lost or ruined in one of the vast inundations that were a depressingly regular feature of fen life until efficient drainage was realised.[150]

At the end of January the enemy reappeared, and a Boston pink making for Sunderland was intercepted by a privateer off Bridlington. The pink had three guns, and in a night-fought action its skipper put them to punishing use until his powder ran out. He then saved his ship by running it ashore near Hornsea.[151]

On the evening of February 2 and all through the following day intermittent heavy gunfire from the sea was heard in Boston, rumoured to be the *Sweepstakes* engaged in a duel with three privateers. Butler also confirmed that he had received and posted up a Royal Declaration in the town, exhorting men to join the Navy, but a month later he complained that while this had produced a few recruits there was no Vice-Admiral nor deputy available to enlist them.[152]

The continuance of the convoy system ensured that in the following months privateers had to work harder for leaner pickings. Throughout May shipping was paralysed when a Dutch battle fleet of 48 men-of-war and numerous attendant vessels appeared off Aldeburgh, and it appears to have sailed at least as far north as Saltfleet before leaving the coast. On June 8, fifteen colliers waiting for convoy in the Boston Deep were daringly attacked by a lone privateer, but with the help of Butler's hard-worked custom boat it was driven off; four of the colliers getting themselves run aground in the process.[153]

At this point, six months short of the termination of the war, Butler's reports peter out. It seems likely that in terms of shipping lost Boston suffered less than it had done in the previous conflict. The war was widely unpopular, not least with the mercantile interests. In the apt words of a leading modern naval historian, it was 'impolitic, unnecessary, and inglorious',[154] and faced with Parliamentary opposition Charles had to conclude a separate peace in February 1674, leaving the French to go it alone. On land the Dutch looked for salvation to the leadership of a taciturn and introverted young man who was later to become the Nemesis of the Stuart dynasty. William, Prince of Orange and eventually King of

England, opened his country's dykes to the sea and Louis's invading armies squelched to a halt.

Dislike of the war did not arise wholly out of disrupted commerce. There were also those that hated the thought of being allied to an autocratic Catholic power against a small Protestant republic. After the war this distaste took concrete form with some groups illegally shipping out of England to enlist in William's army. In June 1674 forty men under a Major Coney and a lieutenant embarked in the *Elizabeth* of Spalding and ignoring the expostulations of the customs officer there, set sail for Holland. Coney is a Boston name of long standing, and it is possible that this particular holder of it came from the town. Again, in the following October, another eighty potential soldiers were reported as having departed in a Boston ship that had picked them up by night in the marshes between Boston and Spalding.[155] The Roundhead flame still burned in the Fens.

Memorandum that all the charge of the forenamed beacons are to be at the costs and charge of the Maier and Burgessies of Boston and to be sett up by such men as have taken them of the Maier and Burgessies to sett up for the some of iiij^li whose names are hereunder written and to be paid quartelly.

> firste   Anthonie Thacker
>   Thomas Harrington
>   Henry Wardall &
>   his brother in lawe.

SURVEY OF SEAMARKS IN 1580

Volume I of the Boston Corporation Minutes contains (f.194) an account of a survey of seamarks carried out by Corporation representatives in 1580. The text is given below. It almost certainly constitutes the earliest detailed outline of navigation aids placed in the Wash.

Burgus de   Memorandum that the viij day of Auguste anno dni
Boston   1580 & xxij^{do} Rene Elizabethe, Richard Draper Maior, Richard Brigge Thomas Doughtie & George Earle Alldermen, Roger Cockes Searcher, taken with them Regnolld Bell of Boston Mr. of a shippe called the William of Boston, Willm Vicar alias Vicars Mr. of a shippe called the Hasprie of Yarmouthe & John Person Mr. of a shippe called the [blank in MS.] of Blackney did goe downe to vewe as well the state of the beacons & See markes now standinge as allso the decay or wante of Beakons or See markes wherewth the Maior and Burgessies of Boston in the countie of Lincolne be chargeable according to the quenes ma^{ties} graunte to them graunted, ytt is thought mete that the firste beacon nexte to Boston at westwarde herne, the second Beacon called Scull Beacon, the third Beacon called Scelpe horn Beacon nowe standeth be repaired where they doe nowe stand, allso that it is necessarie that there be a beacon of newe set up in the mydway between Skelphorne beacon and the elbowe beacon at Storie hawe wch beacon to be newe sett up shalbe the fourth beacon. Allso that the elbowe Beacon beinge the Beacon would be made of a greater and longer tree & kept wth a greater Bushe in the toppe and the same elbowe Beacon to be made wth a can as tyme shall serve. Allso that the southe clay Beacon alias Romefourthe beacon shalbe removed and kepte narre the depe wch southe clay beacon shalbe the vj Beacon. Allso that the seaventhe beacon called northe clay alias Cleybeacon is to be standing and kepte where it standethe. Allso that their be another beacon beinge the viijth beacon newelye sett up betweene north beacon & hye horne att a place a little above lucklowe and their mayneteyned. Allso the ixth beacon at the hye horne be contynued and kepte where it nowe standethe. Allso that the xth beacon be set of newe one the mayn beneathe Boston in Benyngeton & their repaired for the safegarde of the passingers at Skull rigge. Allso yt the xjth and laste Beacon be newlie erected & sett on the longe sand alias Southe Sande and their repaired, wch beacons soe repaired be thoughte to be Seemarkes sufficiente by the opinion of the thre maisters above written.

Yet they thinke it necessarie as tyme shall serve to sett and kepe a can upon the knok, and this be sufficiente in all respects of the charge of the Maior and Burgessies of Boston extendinge to the furtheste parte of their liberties for avoydinge danger of eny traveller.

continued opposite

NOTE ON THE BOSTON PORT BOOKS

The institution whereby customs duties are rendered to the Exchequer was first generally established in the time of Edward I. During the early years of the reign of Elizabeth I a tightening up of the system took place in order to prevent the Crown from being defrauded of its revenues, and this gave rise, in 1565, to the inauguration of Port Books. They consisted of parchment books of a registered number of folios issued in metal boxes to the customers of every port. All transactions of these officials were entered therein and the books were returned to the Exchequer annually, when new books were issued. This practice continued until the administrative development of the customs system rendered their return obsolete, and their use was ended by Treasury Order in 1799.

The books which still survive, in varying states of preservation, are now lodged in the Public Record Office. Those concerning Boston commence at Easter 1565 and terminate at 5 January 1775. They are catalogued in PRO Lists 11/88 and 11/89, pp. 99-110 and 92-106 respectively. A total of 469 books exist, none of which exceeds 33 folios in extent. The average is 8 folios and the total number of folios comprising the whole run is 3976. Given that the majority of these are written on both sides, the sobering fact emerges that until nearly 8000 pages of MS. are transcribed and analysed nothing can be written which can lay claim to approach being a definitive commercial history of the port of Boston. To date the only inroads made upon this material are those of Dr. Hinton and the present writer.

It will be noted that the Boston books span a period of 210 years. All of these years are covered either by a coastal or foreign trade book, or both, with the exception of gaps which amount to a total of almost 56 years. For the time-saving convenience of future researchers a breakdown of this period for which books are *not* extant is given hereunder.

Mich. 1567 – Mich. 1568	Xmas 1628 – Xmas 1629
Easter 1589 – Mich. 1591	Xmas 1635 – Easter 1637
Mich. 1593 – Mich. 1594	Mich. 1637 – Xmas 1638
Mich. 1595 – Mich. 1598	Xmas 1640 – Midsummer 1660
Mich. 1603 – Mich. 1604	Xmas 1661 – Xmas 1666
Easter 1606 – Xmas 1607	Xmas 1670 – Xmas 1671
Xmas 1608 – Easter 1609	Xmas 1701 – Xmas 1702
Mich. 1609 – Xmas 1609	Xmas 1709 – Midsummer 1710
Xmas 1613 – Mich. 1614	Xmas 1733 – Xmas 1734
Mich. 1615 – Xmas 1615	Midsummer 1735 – Xmas 1735
Xmas 1618 – Xmas 1622	Midsummer 1741 – Midsummer 1746
Xmas 1624 – Mich. 1626	Midsummer 1750 – Xmas 1750

BOSTON SHIPS AND MASTERS 1660 - 1673

Except for where otherwise noted the following list has been compiled from Boston's overseas trade Port Books, 1660-73, referred to in the main narrative. The tons burthen of each ship, where ascertainable, is given in brackets. The entry of this detail in the Port Books was required by law, but in Boston's case it appears to have been disregarded after 1667.

Amity (30)	Jeremiah Waller 1660, 61, 68, 70.
Adventure	William Ryley 1670. Matthew Murford 1670.
Blessing[1]	
Charity	William Ryley 1660.
Charles	William Full 1667, 68.
Desire	Thomas Saunderson 1668. Richard Cordell 1670. John Parkinson 1673.
Elizabeth (30)	Samuel Burdis 1660, 61, 67, 68. William Young 1668. Edward Thompson 1670. Edward Jackson 1670.
Happy Entrance[2]	William Full 1670.
Hope	John Robinson 1667. Robert Woods 1668. Matthew Coppin 1670. Edward Thompson 1673.
Hopewell	Thomas Chaplin 1670.
John	William Otter 1660, 61.
John and Elizabeth[3] (30)	James Sneath 1661.
John and Francis	Matthew Coppin 1668. Minard Kartenson[4] 1673.
John and Sarah	John Blunke 1668.
John and Thomas[5] (30)	Edward Mallery 1661. Richard Covell 1664.[6]
Lamb[7]	Conrad Crawford 1667. Daniel Robinson 1668.
Lennox	Thomas Chaplin 1667, 68.
Matthew	Thomas Chaplin 1668. Matthew Murford 1670.
New Exchange[8]	
Prince (30)	Robert Wood 1660, 61.
Providence (70)	Matthew Burchenall 1664.[9] Thomas Rutland 1668.
Speedwell	Richard Clay 1670.
Swallow (20)	John Martin 1660, 61, 67, 68, 70.
Tabitha (20)	William Ryley 1660, 61, 70.
Thomas and John[10]	Thomas Chaplin 1666.
William (36)	Thomas Rutland 1660, 61.

See foot of page 44 for relevant notes.

A B B R E V I A T I O N S (AS USED IN 'NOTES AND SOURCES')

AASR	Associated Architectural and Archaeological Societies Reports and Papers.
BCA	Boston Corporation Archives.
BCM	Boston Corporation Minutes.
BM	British Museum.
CAM	Calendar of the Committee for the Advance of Money 3 vols. 1888.
CCC	Calendar of the Committee for Compounding 5 vols. 1889-92.
CJ	Commons Journals.
Clarke	H. Clarke, *Charters of the Borough of Boston* 1825.
CSPD	Calendar of State Papers, Domestic.
DNB	Dictionary of National Biography.
HBS	History of Boston Series.
Hinton	R.W.K. Hinton, *The Port Books of Boston* 1601-1640 (Lincoln Record Society, Vol. 50, 1956).
HMC	Historic Manscripts Commission.
LJ	Lords Journals.
Maddison	A.R. Maddison, *Lincolnshire Pedigrees* 4 vols. 1902 - 06.
ORMP	Official Return of Members of Parliament. 1878.
PRO	Public Record Office.
PT	Pishey Thompson, *History of Boston* (1856 edition).
Venn	J. &. J. A. Venn, *Alumni Cantabrigiensis* 4 vols. 1922 - 27 Other sources are quoted in full in the references.

Notes relating to previous page.

1. CSPD 1671-2, 239.
2. Lost to privateer, Feb. 1673.   CSPD 1672-3, 519.
3. Purchased Rotterdam Feb. 1661. PRO E.190:396/9, f.1 verso.
4. An alien. He appears earlier in 1673 as master of the *Fortune* of Fredrikstadt, in from Norway after having previously been forced ashore at 'Sollaby' and stranded.
5. A pink, purchased Rotterdam, July 1661. PRO E.190:396/9, f.3 verso.
6. CSPD 1667-8, 215.
7. Lost en route to Rotterdam, Nov. 1668.
   PRO E.190:396/17, ff. 3 verso, 4 recto.
8. CSPD 1672-3, 113.
9. PRO SP.29/107.
10. A collier. Lost to privateer in the Humber, July 1666.
    CSPD 1665-6, 544.

NOTES AND SOURCES

1. E. Carus-Wilson, *The Medieval Trade of the Ports of the Wash*, pub. *Medieval Archaeology*, VI-VII, 185-6, 189. *The Itinerary of John Leland* 1535-1543 ed. L. T. Smith (1910) IV, 114, 181-2; V, 34. PT, 62-3.

2. Clarke, 1, 13-17. (Note: The year of Henry's Charter is erroneously interpreted here as 1546). BCA, 1/A/1, 2. PT, 272-5. J. R. Tanner, *Tudor Constitutional Documents* 1485-1603 (1951), 103-7.

3. Clarke, 2-4, 30, 37-8. In the 18th and early 19th century the fine for attaining freemanship was considerably increased. See PT, 306-7. Saltney, or Salteney, was a salters' settlement in Sutterton Marsh (HBS II, 4).

4. 13 Eliz. I, c.13.

5. BCM, I, f.113 verso.

6. CSPD 1547-1580, 32. His predecessor and original Recorder of Boston in the Charter year of 1545 was Richard Goodrych (BCM,I,f.1). There is no local note of Cecil's accession as its time falls within a one year gap in the Corporation Minutes. A brief entry explains the break in continuity thus: '1551. Henry Foxe Maior. This man toke home with hym all his pamplets of assemblies and so was lost and not restored'. (BCM,I,f.9). Both Cecil and Clinton fulfilled their obligation to the Corporation through their entitlement to appoint a deputy. For Cecil's patent in this respect see Calendar of Patent Rolls, Edward VI, Vol. IV, 337, and for a dispute over his right see HMC *Salisbury* I, 108. In January 1556(7) the Corporation 'agrede yt Mr Cecil shall have a patent sealde of iiij marks (if he will) and all his averages. And yt mast. Smyth shall be ye Recorder of this Towne' (BCM, I,f.25 verso). In 1571 the deputation of both Recorder and High Steward devolved upon one man, Stephen Thimoldby. (BCM, I,f.115 recto and verso).

7. BCM,I,ff. 111 verso, 112, 114 verso.

8. PRO E.190:387/10, 388/1, 388/2, 388/3.

9. These were the *Matthew*, 16 tons, *Margaret* (16), *James* (20), *Bull* (10), *Magdalen* (8), *Mary Anne* (50), and *Swan* (36). The two latter are the overseas traders.

10. BCM,I,ff. 114 recto and verso, 115, 116 verso. The first two of these folios contain a copy of a lengthy letter sent by the Corporation to Audley, and it is this which affords an insight into the haggling which followed the request for an export licence. Pishey Thompson prints the text, with minor alterations and deletions, on p.96 of his work. He gives it merely as a curiosity and footnotes that its purport is obscured by too many words. This is not the case, and his incomprehension was probably conditioned by his just (p.67) having chronicled the date of Boston's Admiralty Charter as 1568; an antedating error of five years.

11. BCM,I,ff. 118 recto and verso, 119 verso, 120.

12. Clarke, 18-23. Boston's Admiralty powers were eventually abrogated by the Municipal Corporations Reform Act of 1835.

13. BCA, 1/B/1,f.50. Tobias Gentleman, *England's way to win wealth &c.* reprinted in *Social England Illustrated* (An English Garner Series, 1903), pp. 245-71.

14. BCA, 1/B/1, ff. 55, 57 recto and verso. BCM,I,ff. 133 verso, 136 verso. HMC *Salisbury* II, 51.

15. BCM,I, ff. 165 recto and verso, 170 verso, 171. HMC *Salisbury* II, 315.

16. HMC *Salisbury* IV, 315-17.

17. HMC *Salisbury* XVII, 169, 593. BCM,I, ff. 406, 407 recto and verso, 410 recto and verso, 411 verso, 412 verso. The stranding of large cetaceans on the Lincolnshire coast seems to have been more frequent in the 17th century than today. The Boston Corporation Minutes contain several references to such events.

18. BCM,I, f.351 verso.

19. BCM, I, ff. 134 verso, 135. Maddison, 50. Audley had been raised from common councillor to alderman of Boston on 30 April 1571. (BCM,I,f. 106).

20. See Appendix I.

21. HMC 11*th Report* III, 288-9. I am indebted to Mr. Michael Winton of King's Lynn for supplying me with information on the contents of Lynn's Admiralty Charter.

22. CSPD 1663-64, 224, 389. BCA 2/B/2. BCM III,f. 447 verso. For a photographic reproduction and transcription of the names appended to the lighthouse petition see E. M. Calvert, *The History of Hunstanton Lighthouse* (1939), 14, 54-5. The patent for the lighthouses became vested in the Bodham family of King's Lynn, and toll-dues on their behalf were collected in Lynn, Boston, Wisbech, and Wells. (Calvert, 22, 33, 39).

23. HMC *Salisbury* V, 393.

24. H. Hall, *A History of the Customs Revenue in England . . .to* 1827 (2 vols. 1888) II, 245.

25. Hinton, 19 *et.seq.* It may be noted that the same author's monograph, *Dutch Entrepot Trade at Boston, Lincs.,* 1600-40 (The Economic History Review, Sec. Series, Vol. IX, No. 3, 1957, pp. 467-71) supplements his edition of the Boston Port Books.

26. CSPD 1635-36, 8. 1637, 378.

27. HBS, VII.

28. Hall, op.cit., II, 248.

29. G. M. Hipkin, *Social and Economic Conditions in the Holland Division of Lincolnshire,* 1640-1660, 194-97. Published in AASR, XL.

30. PRO E. 190:396/8,9,10,11,12,14,16,17. 397/2, 3. It will be noticed that 1665, 1666, and 1672, the peak years of the second and third Dutch Wars, are among those for which no books survive. For a general account of the books see Appendix II.

31. The three officers were the controller, the customer or collector, and the searcher. A fourth, the surveyor, existed until the great farming out of the customs in 1605. Surveyors books for Boston survive for the years 1594-5, 1600-01, 1601-02, 1602-03, and 1604-05.

32. PRO E.190:397/2.

33. Hall, op.cit., I, 183-4.

34. See Appendix III.

35. Pinks were characterised in their hull design by a marked 'tumble-home' and narrow stern. Depending upon their size they carried ship, brig, or sloop rigging. Sketches, based upon Fredrik Henrik af Chapman, *Architectura Navalis Mercatoria* (1768) are given of the other types named.

36. Hinton, 8.

37. Ibid., 254-321.

38. W. Camden, *Britannia,* ed. R. Gough (1789) II, 224. J. A. Clarke, *Fen Sketches* (1852), 70.

39. The Port Books log 27 timber ships incoming from Norway in 1661, 21 in 1670. Between 1601-1640 the highest figures recorded are 15 in 1634 and 16 in 1640.

40. PRO E.190:396/9, ff. 1 verso, 3 verso.

41. Hinton, xxxiv. HBS, V, 6.

42. BCM, III, f. 476.

43. Hinton, xxxvi.

44. CSPD 1665-66, 209. Over a century earlier we find the Duchess of Suffolk writing to Cecil that she was having a ship fitted out at Boston. (CSPD 1547-1580, 30).

45. CSPD 1672, 583.

46. HBS, VII, 32. CSPD 1653-54, 502, 517, 574. 1654, 569. 1655-56, 414. Walter Blith, *The English Improver Improved* (1652) quoted by H. C. Darby, *The Draining of the Fens* (1956), 86.

47. CSPD 1663-64, 142-3.

48. BCM, II, 38.

49. HBS, VII, 33.

50. CSPD 1651, 435. 1651-2, 65. An entry in the Corporation Minutes of 10 June 1653 (III, f. 403) records the sum of £2 voted to 'Mr. More for soliciting on the behalf of Linn and Boston for convoyes for the Sea Trade'. He may have been Joseph More, 'Dr. of Physick' and Lord of Townend Manor, Spalding, who was a county committee member during the Protectorate.

51. BCM, III, f. 399.

52. CSPD 1652-3, 540, 543, 545.

53. Ibid., 206.

54. CSPD 1654, 102, 103, 109, 225, 362, 555, 556.

55. Ibid., 482.

56. CSPD 1656-6, 514, 538. 1656-7, 470, 480, 503, 536. 1657-8, 452, 502.

57. CSPD 1656-7, 232.

58. Ibid., 552.

59. Ibid., 372. 1658-9, 311.

60. HBS, VII, 29-33.

61. BCM, III, f. 400 recto and verso.

62. Firth and Rait, *Acts and Ordinances of the Interregnum* 1642-1660, II, 972, 981. The six named are Thomas Law, John Tilson, Samuel Cust, John Whiting, John Naylor, and Bankes Anderson. For biographical details of all save Naylor, see HBS, VII, 48-57. Both he and Anderson were curates of Boston. The vicar, Anthony Tuckney, was not present. An account of the clerical position in the town at this time is given in the next chapter.

63. *The Journal of George Fox* ed. Norman Penney, 2 vols., (1911) I, 261-2.

64. DNB, LXI, 102.

65. PRO SP.18/183. CSPD 1658-9, 194-6. HMC *5th Report*, 146. DNB, LXIII, 247. The other five Boston signatories were Thomas Tooley, John Tilson, John Whiting, John Naylor, and Bankes Anderson.

66. HBS, VII, 28, 29, 55. CSPD 1655, 320, 324. PT, 243, 454-5. Lincoln Record Society (Parish Registers) I, 81, 89. III, 106, 142. Samuel Whiting was born in 1597 and married Elizabeth St. John at Boston in 1629. Pishey Thompson says (p.430) that she was the daughter of Lord Chief Justice Oliver St. John who was related to Cromwell. As Oliver St. John was born about 1598 this does not seem likely. Nor do the family details of St. John given in the DNB bear out Thompson's contention.

67. HBS, VII, 31-33.

68. CSPD 1654, 219. 1655, 320, 324.

69. CJ, VI, 611. CSPD 1650, 565. 1651, 32. CCC, 1503-4.

70. *Records of the Cust Family* 1479-1700, comp. Lady Elizabeth Cust (1898), 217-220.

71. J. Willcock, *Life of Sir Henry Vane the Younger* (1913), 297. W. H. Dawson, *Cromwell's Understudy* (1938), 376.

72. BCM, III, f. 410 verso. The entry reads that the present was made to 'Maior Generall Lambert his Lady'. Pishey Thompson (p.92) transcribes this as 'Major-general Lambert *and* his lady'. There is no evidence that Lambert himself ever visited Boston.

73. A pedigree giving the main ramifications of this 'cousinage' was first set out by M.Moore in his *The family of Carre of Sleaford* in 1863 and has since been reprinted in H. Dalton, *History of the Wrays of Glentworth* (1880-81) vol. II, and in J. W. F. Hill, *Tudor and Stuart Lincoln* (1956), p.127. See also D. Brunton and D. H. Pennington, *Members of the Long Parliament* (1954), 71.

74. CSPD 1650, 479. 1651, 13. 1654, 228, 286. BCM, III, ff.397, 402 verso, 410 verso 423, 429 verso. BM, Thomason E. 805 (6): *A List of Knights and Burgesses elected to serve in the next Parliament*, July 12, 1654. Willcock, *op cit.*, 266, 328.

75. BM, Thomason 669 f. 19 (3): *A Catalogue of the Names of the Members of the last Parliament*, June 22, 1654. Another of the Lincolnshire representatives, Humphrey Walcott, had been resident in Boston in 1642 but by 1654 had moved to Lincoln (HBS, VII, 56-7).

76. S.R. Gardiner, *The Constitutional Documents of the Puritan Revolution* 1625-1660 (1906),408. The legislation actually increased Lincolnshire's overall representation. Hitherto it had returned two members for Lincoln, Boston, Grantham, Stamford, and Grimsby, plus two for the county; a total of twelve. It now had sixteen: ten for the county, two for Lincoln and one each for the remaining boroughs.

77. BCM,III, f.419. BM,Thomason E. 805(6). HBS, VII,50.

78. BM, Thomason E. 498(5): *A Perfect List of the Names of the several Persons returned to serve in this Parliament*, Sept. 1656. CJ, VI, 424-6.

79. HBS, VII, 52. BCM,III, f.429 verso. J. Adair, *Roundhead General* (1969), 206.

80. Browne Willis, *Notitia Parliamentaria* (1750) III, 290. For Mussenden see HBS VII, 54.

81. BM, Thomason 669 f.21 (43): *A Catalogue of the Members of this present Parliament*, 2 June 1659. Thomason 669 f. 24 (37): *A True and Perfect Catalogue of the Secluded Members of the House of Commons sitting 16 March* [1660].

82. CSPD 1659-60, 15, 16, 24, 38, 44, 52, 53, 75, 77, 91, 94, 95, 99-100, 117, 563. HBS, VII, 1, 2, 4, 6, 7, 9, 10, 12, 13, 15, 16, 18, 19, 20, 24, 32, 46, 47.

83. BM, Egerton MSS, 2541 f.362, printed in AASR, I, (New Series) 217-19.

84. HMC 10*th Report*, VI, 206. *Bath*, II, 121, 137. CSPD 1659-60, 105, 195.

85. BM, Thomason E. 765(9) : *A Perfect List of the Parliament begun at Westminster*, 25 April 1660. HBS, VII, 16-21, 51, 53. PT, 451, erroneously gives *Sir* Thomas Hatcher. Hatcher was never thus honoured. Thompson was probably distracted by using a list also containing the name of Sir Thomas Meres, who sat for Lincoln. For King's activities in the Parliament and a list of the legislation on which he, Irby, and Hatcher sat, see A. A. Garner, *Colonel Edward King* (1970), 25-30, 59-52.

86. *Perfect Occurrences*, May 11-18, 1660. (BM, Burney Collection 54a). *The Diurnal of Thomas Rugg* 1659 - 1661 (Camden Soc., 3rd Series, XCI, 84). For Welby's background see HBS VII, 57.

87. ORMP, I, 524. BCM, III, f.460 verso. The cost of providing 'wind musick', ale, tobacco, and other ceremonies and junketings at the election amounted to £102. 9s. 5½d. (Lincs. Archives Office, *Ancaster*, 13/B/1b).

88. BCM, II, ff. 284 verso, 285. Pishey Thompson, in his list of High Stewards (p.458) carelessly mingles father and son by giving *Montagu* Earl of Lindsey as High Steward in 1634.

89. Since 15 October 1660 (BCM,III, f.452). For the Bertie family see AASR, XX, and E. H. D. Willoughby, *Chronicles of the House of Willioughby de Eresby* (1896).

90. ORMP, I, 524.

48

91. Maddison, 990-91. Venn, IV, 237. PRO, SP. 29/9. HMC *Pepys*, 286, 303. CSPD 1665-66, 164. Thory's statement that the Parliament had taken away his estate leads one to expect that the records of the Committee for Compounding might contain some reference to him. However, the only Thomas Thory touched upon there came from the Partney branch of the family, and he died in 1645. (CCC, 1853. G. G. Walker, *Historical Notes of Partney* (1898), 95-6).

92. CJ, VIII, 251, 416, 421, 458, 484. Page 484 records the judgement in which Thory is given his title of Major. It was later transcribed into the Corporation Minutes (III, f.499) where although the word 'Major' is clearly written, Pishey Thompson saw fit to render it, with doubtful emphasis, as 'Mayor' in a footnote to a list of MPs. given on page 451 of his book. Through this Thory becomes a Mayor of Boston in the Victoria County History of Lincolnshire, II, 287.

93. BCM,II, f.225. CJ,I, 893. ORMP, I, 476. J. H. Sacret, *The Restoration Government and the Municipal Corporations* published in *The English Historical Review*, XLV (1930), 232-59, gives a general discussion of the election disputes of the period.

94. BCM,III, f. 324 verso. The Corporation presumably carried out its elections by ballot. From 1620 onwards there are references to a bag and bullets being handed on in the mayoral induction proceedings.

95. CJ, VIII, 292. In 1711 a disputed by-election return arose at Boston and the judgements of 1628 and 1663 were quoted in argument to the Commons investigating committee. It decided that the right of Parliamentary election in the borough lay with 'the mayor, aldermen and common councill and freemen, resident in the said borough and paying scot and lot'. At this time the franchise entitlement was computed as extending to 200 inhabitants. In yet another disputed Boston return, in 1719, the resolution of 1711 was reaffirmed with an added rider further defining the voting freemen as constituting only those who held their freemanship by birth or servitude. (ORMP, II, 21, 41. Thomas Carew, *An Historical Account of Rights of Elections of the several Counties, Cities, and Boroughs of Great Britain* (1755), 65-68).

96. BCA, 5/B/1/1.

97. Hearth Tax Returns for 1665 (PRO E. 179. 140/754) accord Boston 518 dwellings, Pishey Thompson, (p.104) without quoting the whereabouts of his source gives the population in 1678 as 2070 based upon inhabitants and sojourners assessed to the Poll-tax granted to Charles II, 'all said to be included'. Regarding this it should be noted that the Poll Tax Act of 1667 (19 Car. II, c.i.) has provision for exempting the poor and persons under 16.

98. BCM,III, f.552 verso.

99. The Corporation Minutes contain no note of the election, but on 14 August 1666 Barkham and Harcourt (in company with Irby's son, who was then 16 years old) underwent the necessary prerequisite formality of being made freemen (BCM, III, f.505 verso). The election writ was issued on 21 September (CJ,VIII, 626) and the return made on 26 October (ORMP, I, 524). For Barkham's pedigree see Maddison, 84-7.

100. Anthony Wood, *Athenae Oxoniensis* (1721) I, 393, II, 807. DNB, XXIV, 321-2. LIX, 134. W. Cobbett, *Parliamentary History of England* (1808) IV, 858-59.

101. *The Genealogist*, I (Old Series) 242. Maddison, 737. CCC, 1296. CAM, 1072. HBS, VII, 25, 54-5.

102. Maddison, 1041. CCC, 1379. CAM, 1073. Venn, IV, 324.

103. Maddison, 1022. CCC, 954. CAM, 727. LJ, V, 127. BM, Thomason: *Mercurius Aulicus*, 16 April 1643.

104. BCM,III, ff. 476 recto and verso, 477. Pishey Thompson (pp. 93, 434, 455) wrongly gives *Andrew* Slee as replacing Preston in the mayoralty in 1662.

105. PT, 768.

106. Maddison, 104.

107. Who was not Andrew's father as maintained by Pishey Thompson (p.434-5). Hinton (pp. xxix, xlii) following Thompson, repeats the error. Thompson's genealogy of Baron is generally incorrect. See Maddison, 103-5.

108. He was made freeman on 25 October 1606 (BCM,I, f. 420).

109. BCM,II, ff. 12 verso, 15, 26. DNB, III, 265. PT, 414. HBS, V, 11.

110. BCM,III, f. 474. ORMP,I, 536.

111. BCM,III, ff. 474 verso, 475 verso. Venn, II, 299. Maddison, 1022. DNB, XLIII, 126-7. A. O. Barron, *Northamptonshire Families* (1906) II, 246. ORMP, I, 490, 530.

112. BCM,III, f.497 verso.

113. Thomas Blore, *History and Antiquities of Rutland* (1811), 69, 70. Barron, *op. cit.* Victoria County History, *Northants.*, III, 133-4. Maddison, 251, 737. CJ, VIII, 18.

114. See G. F. Trevallyn Jones, *The Composition and Leadership of the Presbyterian Party in the Convention* (published in *The English Historical Review*, LXXIX (1964), 307-54, for the background to this.

115. HBS, VII, 48, 51-2, 56. BCM,III, ff. 367, 439 verso, 449. In late 1658 Dr. Tuckney appears to have been of the opinion that Boston was in a religious decline and that its magistracy was sleepy and careless (HBS, V, 27).

116. Dr. Williams's Library: Wilson MS., I,i, f. 254. Wilson simply embroiders the c.1774 MS. of Josiah Thompson (DWL, MS. 38. 9. ff. 112-13) whose brief account of Boston Presbyterianism derives from 'the Private Papers of one belonging to that Congregation which go no further back than 1698'.

117. CSPD 1672-3, 261. A. G. Matthews, *Calamy Revised* (1934), 453. W. E. Foster, *The Plundered Ministers of Lincolnshire*, 76-78.

118. Dr. Williams's Library: Wilson MS., I, ff. 262-66. Wilson's account of Boston's Baptist congregation appears to have been composed from material scattered in Adam Taylor's *The history of the English General Baptists*, 2 vols. 1818. CSPD 1672-3, 94. For biographical material on Grantham see Edmund Oldfield, *Historical Account of Wainfleet* (1829), 353-64, PT, 436-7. DNB, XXII, 410.

119. BCM, III, f. 477. His tenure was periodically reaffirmed (BCM,III, ff. 497, 504 verso, 536). Pishey Thompson, in his list of Admiralty Court Judges (p.459) incorrectly gives 1652 as the year of Lake's initial appointment.

120. CSPD 1672, 536, 538.

121. Larzer Ziff, *The Career of John Cotton* (1956) 40. *The Camden Miscellany* IV, (1859) ix. Maddison, 577, DNB, XXXI, 409, XXXVII, 27. Supplement II, 69. *Dictionary of American Biography*, VI, 394.

122. PRO, S.P.29/107.

123. CSPD 1664-65, 191, 214, 216, 368.

124. CSPD 1665-66, 542, 544, 550, 556, 561.

125. CSPD 1666-67, 164.

126. CSPD 1665-66, 553, 573. 1666-67, 26, 338. The *Truelove* was a sixth rate of 60 men and 12 guns. Its human cargo was to be distributed among the King's ships at Yarmouth. (*The Rupert and Monck Letter Book* 1666, pub. Navy Records Society, Vol. CXII (1969), 12, 66-7).

127. CSPD 1666-67, 49. W. D. Fellowes, *Historical Sketches of Charles I, Cromwell, Charles II, &c.* (1829) quoted PT, 93.

128. I base this assertion upon an examination of parish registers and/or local histories of the main population centres of the county.

129. CSPD 1664-65, 44, 513. 1666-67, 191. *Archaeologia*, XXXVII, (1857), 1-22.

50

130. BCM, I, f. 395 recto and verso. PRO, SP. 45/11.
131. Maddison, 230. AASR, VII, 60-70. ORMP,I, 524, 542, 548. CSPD 1671-72, 135, 149. BCM,III, ff. 502, 505 verso, 538 recto and verso, 539 verso. *Register of Admissions to Gray's Inn*, ed. J. Foster (1889), 135. *Letters addressed to Sir Joseph Williamson in* 1673-1674, pub. 2 vols. by the Camden Society in 1874, I, 2.
132. CSPD 1671, 337, 477, 547, 577. 1671-72, 83, 92, 600.
133. CSPD 1667, 30, 92, 107, 130.
134. CSPD 1667-8, 214-15.
135. CSPD 1671, 133.
136. PRO, E.190:396/17 ff. 3 verso, 4. CSPD 1671, 565.
137. CSPD 1671-2, 239, 240, 286.
138. BCM, III, ff. 476, 510 verso.
139. CSPD 1671-2, 276, 349, 461, 492, 529, 542. 1672, 16, 50, 115, 271-2.
140. CSPD 1672, 3, 35.
141. Ibid., 266, 307, 278.
142. Ibid., 307, 408, 424, *Acts of the Privy Council,* X, (New Series) 1577-1578, 141.
143. PRO, E.190:396/17 f. 1 recto and verso. CSPD 1672-3, 519.
144. CSPD 1672, 438, 470, 498.
145. Ibid., 560, 642, 661. 1672-3, 9, 15, 47, 160, 556, 594.
146. BCM, IV, f. 23.
147. CSPD 1672-3, 17, 32, 51, 80, 81, 62-3, 69, 75, 85, 141, 149, 171, 182, 247.
148. Ibid., 99.
149. Ibid., 113, 168, 221.
150. Ibid., 380.
151. Ibid., 511-12, 548.
152. Ibid., 461, 519, 596.
153. CSPD 1673, 208, 226, 237, 297, 368, 396, 442.
154. Oliver Warner, *The Navy* (1968), 51.
155. CSPD 1673-5, 378-9. Addenda 1660-85, 441.

INDEX

53